Whispers of the Mind
A Complete Program for Unlocking the Secrets of Your Past Lives

D1007365

Elaine Stephens

1817

Harper & Row, Publishers, San Francisco

New York, Grand Rapids, Philadelphia, St. Louis
London, Singapore, Sydney, Tokyo, Toronto

FIRST EDITION

Library of Congress Cataloging-in-Publication Data

Stephens, Elaine.
    Whispers of the mind.

    Includes bibliographical references.
    1. Reincarnation. 2. Autogenic training. I. Title.
BL515.S742 1990   133.9'01'3   89-45541
ISBN 0-06-250851-2

90 91 92 93 94 BANTA 10 9 8 7 6 5 4 3 2 1

This book is dedicated in
loving memory to my father,
Marshall Dale Bush,
who gave me wings.

"The dead are not powerless.
'Dead' did I say? There is
no death, only a change of
worlds."

—CHIEF SEATTLE, 1855

Contents

Foreword

It was the summer of 1978. My husband and I were returning from a week's vacation at my parents' home in Florida. The family station wagon held our four children, our luggage, and lots of sand. We had done Disney World, visited the beaches, collected shells, and acquired a good tan. We stopped for dinner in a small town I could not even tell you the name of now. Next door to the restaurant was a bookstore.

As I stepped out of the car I said, "Oh good, a bookstore. Let's all go in and get a book for the trip." Entering a bookstore with four kids under twelve is not exactly a quiet, contemplative sort of time. Certainly not dramatic, just a very commonplace, ordinary thing to do. But that day changed my life. As I browsed, my eyes were drawn to a book titled *You Were Born Again to Be Together*. I picked it up, flipped it over, and read the back of the book. It spoke of hypnosis being used to explore past lives. I was hooked. I wanted to know more.

As I read, my mind flashed back to ten years before when I had given birth to my son Michael. Hypnosis had been the anesthetic for his birth. My mind raced, wild with enthusiasm. This same tool, hypnosis, could be used to explore past lives. Within months I traveled from my home in Houston, Texas, to Scottsdale, Arizona, to train in regressive hypnosis with the book's author, Dick Sutphen. I had finally discovered what I wanted to do "when I grew up." I wanted to work with hypnosis. I wanted to understand myself more. It was so easy. There was no mystery. It was something I could take hold of, use, explore with. And so began my own journey.

For years I had read and studied. I had joined organizations and groups, growing disenchanted with time, moving on, needing to know more, needing to understand how and why the mind worked. The key was handed to me in a little town somewhere in Florida on a very ordinary day.

It is my hope that this book will be a key for you to understand your life a little better. I do not offer this information as *the* answer. It is one of many answers, a part of the puzzle, a part of the great mystery called Life

Use what you discover in working with self-hypnosis and past-life exploration to stimulate your curiosity, to find the pieces of your own puzzle. As you discover each piece, hold it in your hand, examine it, and keep moving, looking for more truth, more understanding. Think of your journey as an adventure. Approach it playfully, with an open mind. Trust what comes to you.

Each of us may have lived hundreds of lives, or maybe ten. It doesn't matter how many lives we've lived, or if reincarnation is a figment of our imagination. What matters is how we use the information from our own minds in our life. If you can learn about one fear, one relationship, one question, and use that learning to help yourself, you have done a superlative job. Learn to listen to the whispers of your mind.

Acknowledgments

No one arrives at any destination without the assistance of others, both seen and unseen. My heartfelt thanks go to:

My clients, who have shared their joy, their pain, their courage with me. Each of you has been an integral part of my own learning.

My friends and sharers of the pen, Marj Gurasich and Barbara Riley, two authors who have been my teachers, my inspiration, and my courage when there were deadlines to meet, chapters to rewrite.

Christi Bonds and Gail Lipparelli, who came forward at critical times with invaluable assistance on the manuscript.

Fran Hunter, who generously opened her home in Carson City for the first classes based on this material.

John Rankin, my teacher, who—being the best of teachers—led me to myself.

Joanie Ward, who said to me while in a trance in my office, "This is for you, Elaine. Write a book. Tell people how to explore past lives."

My mother, Elizabeth Bush, who through example taught me that I could accomplish anything.

My family, Larry Bush, Dennis and Holly Bush, Don and Marilyn Webster, who love and support me regardless of what

I write, even though it is said I am "the floppy wheel on the family grocery cart."

My children, Lisa and Michael, who've enjoyed having a mom who was just a little different. And my "other children," Scott and Kelly, who added such joy to my life.

My extended family, Jane Sheffield, Carole and Wayne Morrison, Jan Wingo, Peggy Hampton, Adriana Villareal, Kathy Stimac, Margaret Huber, Melissa Lockwood, Susan Andrade, and Tom Stimac. Blessings to you all, for your love and caring concern through both joyful and difficult times.

The women in my circle, Barbara Pilkington, Dee Totten, Ethyl Sands, Carol Pagonas, Janice Hogan, Linda Kitson, Jo Nollsch, Barbara Doring, Faith Fessenden, Kris Games, Mardelle Pedersen, and Cheryl Harrington, for nourishing the seed of things to come

Mark Salzwedel, my editor at Harper & Row, who with his astute mind and gentle good humor encouraged me to expand the first draft of this manuscript to make it "better and better."

And finally, to the magnificent birch tree that lives beside the pond outside the window where I write.

I hope I see you all . . next time.

Although the first-person stories discussed in this book are true, the names and identifying details of some individuals have been changed in order to protect their privacy.

CHAPTER 1

Why?

Each of us, every single one of us, knows we are special. Intuitively we know there's so much more to us than meets the eye, any eye. And somehow, intuitively, we know within our grasp lies insight into the parts of us that will explain all the dimensions of our being. We are exploring our potential. We are beginning to realize that our mind is the place to begin. We have the ability to understand ourselves so much more fully than we do at this moment. It's an exciting idea, this idea of more, of simple solutions that lie within our own minds, waiting to help us.

We don't need gurus, highly trained specialists, or scholars to guide us. We can guide ourselves. We can take the reins. We have the insight necessary to make changes, to discover our inner courage, to help ourselves.

If we will take time to scrutinize our lives, to look at the clues in our day-to-day existence, we will hear the past echoing forward into the present. We can see a glimmer here, a flash there—provocative little experiences that test our ability to go beyond what we have been told is so. As we begin to entertain the idea that we may have lived before, as we reach into our minds for these other experiences, these moments in time, the distant past and the present, weave into one. As this happens, it's as though a curtain lifts and light shines in. Suddenly, the lesson to be learned is made clear, bringing a sense of relief and freedom.

The process of exploring your past lives involves simple procedures that lead to quantum leaps. The memories are yours. They are readily available. Often we rely too heavily on technology for answers. For some people, life presents extraordinary events that happen within ordinary reality. Charles Lindbergh, during his historic flight, experienced things beyond the ordinary. In his *Autobiography of Values*, he wrote, "In Missouri, at age twenty, I was a disciple of the rising deity of Science, prepared to make daily sacrifices toward a mechanistic future that seemed to hold great benefits for men."

During his thirty-four-hour trip the requirement of staying awake became too much for his physical body. In the eighteenth hour of his journey, he felt himself as "an awareness spreading through space, over the earth and into the heavens, unhampered by time or substance." He became aware of human presences, transparent, riding weightless with him in the plane. His comment on these beings gives one pause for thought. He said it was, "as though I've known all of them before in some past incarnation." "Perhaps," he said, "they are the products of the experience of ages, dwellers of a realm presently closed to the people of our world." Did he have help on that flight from celestial guides, from friends of previous incarnations? We can only wonder.

The human mind works like a computer. It stores vast amounts of information. At a subconscious level we know how many panes of glass are in our living room. We know how many steps it takes us to get from our front door to our car. We know a multitude of things. We can be taken back to the moment of our birth and remember who was in the room, what was said. Unlike a computer, we do not ordinarily possess a retrieval system for this information. But by relaxing, we can remember many things, including other times and places that just might be other lives we have lived.

Once, long ago, each of us saw through the eyes of a magical three-year-old child. We looked at the world without judgment, with a totally open mind. We can learn to see again through those eyes, using the creative part of ourselves that has been so systematically anesthetized by the world we live in. It is said that Napoleon worked out his battle strategies in a sandbox. He said he did this because "imagination rules the world." Each of us can be imaginative, can allow ourselves the luxury of seeing, however briefly, through the eyes of the magical three-year-old we once were.

Some have stated firmly their belief in reincarnation. Gen. George Patton, when asked if he believed in reincarnation replied, "I don't know about other people, but for myself there has never been any question. I just don't think it, I damn well know there are places I've been before, and not in this life." When he assumed his first command in France at the ancient town of Langres, he knew where an old Roman amphitheater was, a drill ground, the forum, and the temples of Mars and Apollo, even though some of these sites no longer existed. He also knew where Caesar had pitched his tent. He had never been to Langres, France, and yet it was as familiar to him as his own hand. We know that in this life he was a brilliant military strategist. Did he acquire these skills in other battles and other times? Can we "know" in that way? Can we give ourselves permission to set our imagination free, to throw off the shackles we have chained ourselves with?

Reincarnation is not a new idea. It dates back to Pythagoras, Plato, and Chuang Tzu, a Taoist living in 300 B.C. It is a tenet of the Hindu and Buddhist religions. However, the common use of the ability to intentionally review one's past lives is a relatively new phenomenon. We in the West have been introduced to this idea, in part, through the trance mediumship of Edgar Cayce, a man with only an eighth-grade education and a simple lifestyle who first came to the world's attention in an article in the *New York Times* in 1910. He possessed the ability to attain a self-induced trance, and while in trance he could diagnose and describe treatments for physical ailments of people he had never met. During the course of his trance readings he began to speak of past lives that were affecting current-life physical and/or emotional problems. He gave detailed accounts of how a past life was affecting the person in the present. Edgar Cayce's work was one of the few known sources available on the subject of reincarnation during the first half of this century.

Popular interest was captured in 1954 when the story of Bridey Murphy was serialized in the *Denver Post,* followed by Morey Bernstein's bestselling book *The Search for Bridey Murphy.* The book was based on hypnotic sessions conducted by Morey Bernstein, a Pueblo, Colorado, businessman, who hypnotized a housewife. In these sessions he probed memories of her early life. As he asked questions, his subject, without specific instructions from him, began speaking of a previous life in Ireland. The details of her past life memories were later debunked by a zealous press. Later, after further research, the details she gave regarding currency and other specifics, were found to be accurate.

A trance medium who more recently spoke matter-of-factly of past lives was Jane Roberts, who channeled all of the Seth books. In her channeled work she often referred to past lives and their effect on the present. Another modern-day author and trance medium whose work is widely known is Ruth Montgomery. Her channeled book, *Here and Hereafter* (1968), specifically deals with reincarnation.

And who was not enchanted in 1970 when the movie *On A Clear Day You Can See Forever,* starring Barbra Streisand, was released. In the movie (based on a Broadway hit play by Alan Jay Lerner), the character Barbra Streisand portrays recalls, while in hypnosis, elaborate tales of court intrigue that involve the other characters in the movie.

The topic of past lives and reincarnation is becoming less bizarre to many people because of the host of books being published on the subject. Considering reincarnation gives us a new perspective from which to view our lives. My own work over the last ten years has clearly demonstrated to me that interest in this subject is growing. Requests for past-life regressions have increased one-hundred-fold during this period. My clients are ordinary people from all walks of life who in the present moment are looking for ways to understand themselves more fully.

Exploring past lives can lead to the release of guilt, bitterness, and self-pity. You can see the parts of the puzzle come together. You can experience yourself as whole and perfect. You learn that each relationship, each experience in your life, has meaning and purpose. As you work with the process, you find mental blocks to your success and happiness removed. You learn to look at your life as an opportunity to be tender and caring, to be your very best. You can gain insight into how to manage your life, to explore your subconscious, and to become aligned with your purpose. To explore your past lives is to be like an embryo, to be involved in your own birth, to be a central figure in the plan for the new being. This is not a psychological process, it is a journey. It is a beginning.

The most important question we can ask begins with why. "Why do I have these feelings?" "Why am I in this relationship?" "Why do I long for so many things, when at times I'm not even sure what they are?" The answers are available; they are forever within us. The key is to reach inside yourself and bring your own answers up, to understand why, and with that understanding, to learn the lesson, we, as our own teachers, have set up. As we discover the pattern to our learning, the purpose of our struggles and joys, we can live our life with more purpose, more awareness. "Why me?" we so often ask. "Did I really create this situation? I can't believe I did." But somehow, for our own reasons, we did create the situations in our life. We can learn from them and move on.

Survival is not the issue. We all survive the major traumas and events in our lives. Think back to the times you amazed yourself with your strength. If someone had asked you the day before such a time, can you handle that, your answer would have been an unequivocal no. And yet, presented with multitudes of difficult situations, you *have* survived, and in most cases have been amazed at your ability to persevere. Survival is our strongest instinct.

Beyond survival, beyond simply doing what must be done, is an inward journey that will provide you with more joy, more awareness, and more personal power than you can possibly imagine. In this journey are the keys to your success at every level. If we are wise and courageous, we choose to make this journey inward, to the center of our being, so that we can live our lives truly in tune with ourselves, fulfilling our unique destiny, loving and being loved.

CHAPTER 2

"I Think I Made That Up"

I think I made that up. I'm not sure I believe in this anyway.

These are phrases I often hear when people experience a past-life regression. It doesn't seem to matter if it is experienced in a private session or a group. It also doesn't seem to matter how dynamic the experience was, how emotion-packed, whether or not the speakers have tears running down their cheeks or are shaking their heads in disbelief at what they have just experienced. If their experience relates to their lives, which it most generally does, that seems to provide even more reasons to doubt the experience. The responses I hear often include statements like, "But I've always been fascinated by World War I, I used to build model planes from that era as a child. I could identify every kind of plane, knew all about them. I probably just used that information. It was already in my subconscious." The speaker didn't realize that the interest from childhood, the compelling need to know about something that had nothing to do with a boy's life on a farm, might have come from his experiences in another lifetime as a pilot.

We find ways to justify, explain away, or not accept the images that come from our minds. The reason people decide to experience a regression is usually because they're curious: they want to know more, they want to understand themselves better. And yet, when the images come into their minds and feelings rise up from another time and place, they immediately begin to explain it away, or simply say, "I'm not sure I believe in this anyway."

Why do we have this fascination with World War I, have a poster of Greece hanging on our wall, love a certain color or style of dress? Where do these likes come from? Why is it that sometimes we meet someone who repels us, who makes us angry simply with their presence? What about the strong attraction for certain people? Why did we see them across a crowded room and want to see more of them?

What about experiences of *déja vu?* In the midst of other activities we are struck with the familiarity of a person or place? Almost everyone has had that experience at one time or another. It's so easy to dismiss the feeling, to think for a fleeting moment how strange it is. We then put that feeling out of our mind and turn to other things.

Could these feelings, these images possibly be a message from our subconscious about our past lives? Are we tapping into Jung's "collective unconscious?" What is it all about? By the time we have this all figured out, we won't be here, so let's not spend our time and energy trying to define it. Let's work with ourselves, with our skepticism. Let's overcome our self doubts. Let's learn to trust ourselves.

Why is it we do not trust what comes from our own mind, the images, the feelings, the strong desires? We begin to search: we read, we attend seminars, workshops, classes. We climb to the top of a multitude of mountains hoping to find a wise man with "our" answer. We are told over and over by the teachers we seek out, "The answer is within you." And yet still we seek, hoping that magically, one golden day the *truth* will be revealed to us. We want so badly to know beyond a shadow of a doubt that we even sit at the feet of those who are not worthy of teaching us, who do not have their own answers, let alone guidance for others. Yet we continue to resist those murmurings from within ourselves, those images that dance before our inner eye, that live within our own consciousness.

Movies and books inundate us with thoughts of reincarnation. The movie *Somewhere in Time* speaks of a love from another life rekindled in the present. It is the story of a man who finds a way to travel back in time to his love. *The French Lieutenant's Woman* cleverly weaves a tale of past love and present frustration. In the movie *Resurrection,* Ellen Burstyn portrays a woman who through a tragedy in her life becomes a healer. The film shows what the world does with her gift. The movie *Close Encounters of the Third Kind* reveals other dimensions, other beings. Our imaginations are constantly stimulated; our hunger for understanding mounts. And yet, given the opportunity to see what wonders lie within our own minds, we doubt. We find it so hard to really believe that these images before our eyes now, these feelings not created by outside stimuli, might in fact be a genuine key to understanding ourselves.

It helps at times to know that many who have gone before us have held reincarnation as part of their belief system. It's hard to feel foolish considering the subject of reincarnation when we realize that many great minds have held this belief. Consider the words of Benjamin Franklin: he said, "I feel as if I was intruding among posterity when I ought to be abed and asleep. I look upon death to be as necessary to the constitution as sleep. We shall rise refreshed in the morning." In a letter Franklin wrote at seventy-nine, he said, "When I see nothing annihilated and not a drop of water wasted, I cannot suspect the annihilation of souls, or believe that [God] will suffer the daily waste of millions of minds ready-made that now exist, and put Himself to the continual trouble of making new ones. Thus, finding myself to exist in the world, I believe I shall, in some shape or other, always exist; and, with all the inconveniences human life is liable to, I shall not object to a new edition of mine, hoping, however, that the *errata* of the last may be corrected." When reporters asked Thomas Edison if he believed in survival after death, he replied: "The only survival I can conceive is to start a new earth cycle again."

Henry Ford has this to say about his beliefs:

"I adopted the theory of Reincarnation when I was twenty-six. . . . Religion offered nothing to the point. . . . Even work could not give me complete satisfaction. Work is futile if we cannot utilize the experience we collect in one life in the next. When I discovered Reincarnation it was as if I had found a universal plan. I realized that there was a chance to work out my ideas. Time was no longer limited. I was no longer a slave to the hands of the clock. . . . Genius is experience. Some seem to think that it is a gift or talent, but it is the fruit of long experience in many lives. Some are older souls than others, and so they know more. . . . The discovery of Reincarnation put my mind at ease. . . . If you preserve a record of this conversation, write it so that it puts men's minds at ease. I would like to communicate to others the calmness that the long view of life gives to us."

Believing in reincarnation is not a prerequisite to exploring your own mind. All you need to do is allow yourself to be open and receptive to your inner self. As you work with the tools presented in the following chapters and have your own experiences, you will gain insight into yourself, and very possibly solutions to some of the situations in your life. Give yourself permission to trust yourself, to see what wonders lie within you. An open mind is the only requirement for success.

CHAPTER 3

The Past Is A Key to the Present

Your mind is the greatest resource you possess. It is the storehouse of everything that has ever happened to you, a treasury of past lives, the fountain of your creativity, your resource for dealing with difficulties in your life. It is your essence. Learning to use your mind creatively is the most wonderful thing you can accomplish for yourself. This is not difficult: the only requirement is that you be willing to trust the images and feelings that come from within you.

A past-life regression can help you learn about the present. The past is your teacher. It can provide you with clues to your relationships. Everyone who has significance in your life has probably been with you before. This is a way for you to learn the purpose of your present involvement. It is an opportunity to enhance an already joyful relationship. One man who experienced a regression regarding his fiancée came out of hypnosis saying, "That won't happen again, will it? I won't lose her again?" The lifetime he had just explored had taken him back to a time when the woman he had just proposed to had been in his life. In that other time, when their love was new, he had proposed. Then, hiking in the mountains, spending precious time together with all the world before them, she had slipped, fallen from a great height, and been killed.

He had come to me for a regression because he had recently spent time re-evaluating his priorities. He had taken an honest look at the fact that when he came home late at night, there was no one there, no one to love. He had decided that perhaps he was now ready to have someone to love in his life. "Maybe," he said, "I can ease up here, turn some of these responsibilities over to others and allow myself to have the time a relationship would require." So he had met and proposed to the woman whose safety now concerned him.

His fear was understandable. It made him aware of why now, in this time, he felt such a need to protect her. She is a competent woman, not someone one would feel a need to protect, and yet those feelings were part of his love for her. Did they come from a past life? Did he just make all that up to justify their rather hasty decision to marry? Could he put that fear, those feelings aside and treasure his time with her now? Would it be short?

"Put those thoughts away," I said. "I don't believe you will lose her in an accident in this life. In the present your love is a gift, a time of being together, an opportunity to have all the moments missed in that other time. That experience wasn't a punishment. It wasn't a way to torture you, but a way for you to grow, to experience life, to realize how fragile life is, how fleeting, and how we must spend it with wisdom now."

This man is a skillful writer; in that other time, he had owned and edited a newspaper. He had immersed himself in his work to deaden the pain from his loss of the woman he loved. By experiencing a regression, he was given clues from his own mind about his current interests and abilities, and more importantly, about the new love in his life.

Were these images from his subconscious? This experience he had just had, was it a fabrication? Or was it his subconscious alerting him to the issues in his life in the present? Maybe he needed to enter this relationship realizing how fragile life is, how time with a loved one is important, even more important than his business. Perhaps his well-devel-

oped writing skills were honed in another life. All he knew
for sure was that he had to write reports, proposals, and letters for his business. It was an ability he possessed that came
easily to him. Maybe his subconscious added the information
about how he had spent the remainder of his life after his
lover's death to bring to his mind the importance of their
time now and the information about writing was only to add
impact to the message.

Exploring the possibility of past lives gives us an opportunity to deal with something that is hauntingly familiar and
then to play a part in our own movie. If a past life is affecting
you now, you have probably satiated yourself with aspects of
that life by reading books, seeing movies, and visiting places
that evoke feelings you have not been able to explain. Did
you have a favorite book as a child? Are you drawn to a specific historical time? By taking a look at your life, you will
know which subject to explore first.

Finding Love

"I really feel that was all made up. It was just like the book
I most loved and read over and over as a child. I just feel it's
too pat, too easy."

We had just finished a group regression and the participants were relating what they learned to the group. I had
directed them to review a past life that would give them insight into a current interest or skill they had. I continued
asking questions of the woman talking, trying to understand
why she was choosing not to believe what had just come from
her own subconscious.

"Does what you've just seen relate in some way to your
current life?" I asked.

"Oh yes," she replied. "But that's why it seems too pat, so
predictable."

"Would you tell me what you experienced, and what the connection is to your present life?"

"Well, in a nutshell," she replied, "what I experienced was a lifetime when I was a small, slight boy, perhaps a gypsy. I was dark-complexioned, unwashed. I was totally responsible for a beautiful Andalusian stallion. The horse was the only thing in my life. I groomed him and I slept curled beneath the manger in his stall. When you directed us to move to an event with another person who was significant in that life, there was just a fleeting awareness of several people in the stable looking over the stall door talking about what a wonderful way I had with the stallion. I was silent, sullen, attuned only to the horse. And then when you moved us forward in time again, something had happened to the stallion and I was alone. I don't know what happened, but I left the people I lived with and just wandered, it seemed. There didn't seem to any significant person, nothing else in my life that mattered but my love and feelings for the horse."

"All right," I said, "how does this relate to now? Are horses part of your professional life, or a hobby? How does it reflect your life now?"

"No, professionally I own a business not related to horses," she said. "But horses are a burning interest of mine, especially European horses. I have helped to establish a registry on the North American continent of these horses. I did all that work because I love those animals so much. I actually don't want to make money with the project, it's a labor of love."

"And you are doubting what you've just experienced?" I asked. "I want you to think about everything you just told me and realize why you were so interested in that book you loved as a child, why you have spent so many hours working on a project without pay. Trust what you've received. It came from your mind, no one else here has experienced what you have. Doesn't it make sense to you that this fits really well, not just sort of, but is like a custom riding boot, perfect only for you? Think about it for awhile, don't dismiss what you've felt as too pat. Watch your dreams tonight, see what other feelings come to the surface with this experience now in your conscious mind."

"I think I see what you're saying," she laughed. "It really is hard to trust the material that comes from our own mind. I'll get better at it with practice, and yes, already it's making more sense reviewing it out loud."

"Good," was my reply. "Trust yourself."

She stayed after class to talk with me further. As we talked I began to realize how really significant these horses were to her. They had also served as an introduction to a very important man in her life. On a trip to Europe she had called on him because of his involvement with these same horses. Their interest in the horses and each other was intense. He canceled his appointments for the remainder of the day. They found themselves enchanted with the conversation and each other.

The rest of the story is yet to be told.

Were these images she received too pat? Did they just serve to reinforce a love she already had? Perhaps meeting this significant man through her love of the horses was her subconscious telling her that this time she would not have to be alone if something happened to her horses. Maybe the message from her mind was, "You can have both now, your love of horses and a special man in your life."

The primary reason to remember your past lives is to have greater awareness of yourself and to have more control and power in your life. Curiosity is a good enough reason to want to begin to explore past lives. Once you begin to have awareness of the richness and variety of information stored within your mind, you will want to dig further, learn more, and use the information to clarify and illuminate your life.

I have found in my work that it is the skeptics who have the most incredible experiences. They will often attend a workshop with a friend, slightly amused to find themselves entertaining the idea that they may have lived before. It is always fun to watch the look on their faces when they come out of hypnosis. They certainly don't leave the room absolutely embracing the concept of reincarnation, but a door has been opened which they can now walk through to explore further.

Learning to Play

"I'm here with a friend. I was really skeptical, and now I'm amazed," one woman told me. "This wasn't at all what I expected." We were winding up another group regression that explored a current interest or skill.

"I wanted to find out about my expertise and interest in golf," she said. "I fully expected to see myself golfing in Scotland. That was my preconceived idea about what I'd experience tonight."

"Oh, and what did you see instead?" I asked.

"It's so strange, I just can't believe this. I saw myself as a man, a traveling peddler. I had a knapsack I carried over my back, walking from village to village selling my wares."

"I'm intrigued. What did this peddler have to do with golf?"

"Absolutely nothing," she said. "But as I walked from village to village, I carried a stick that I used to hit stones with. I was an incredible shot with that stick. Everyone in the villages looked forward to my visits. They bought my wares and asked me to hit the stone to specific targets. I'd stand around and talk with the people. Everyone really liked me. They'd say, "Can you hit the third board from the top of that shed?"

I'd laugh and say, 'Let me see if I can.' They would even make bets on whether or not I could hit it. And I always could. I practiced as I walked from town to town. I amazed myself with my accuracy."

"How's your golf game in this life?" I asked.

She smiled modestly and said. "I'm state amateur champion. And that's really surprising because I only took up golf five years ago."

"I don't know a whole lot about golf," I said, "but it seems to me your accuracy, which I assume is a very necessary ingredient to your success now, was picked up in this other time. How does this relate to now? Close your eyes a moment, take a deep breath, and allow insight to come into your mind."

She did as I asked, and when she opened her eyes she was smiling. "Do you know what else is strange about this? In the lifetime that I just explored, I loved seeing the people. It was so much fun to hit those rocks. It wasn't a contest, I didn't have to do it, it was just fun. It added to my life. One of the things they teach you about golf is that you really have to concentrate. You're not supposed to allow anyone "into your space," as they call it. And you know what's really funny about it? I've never done that. I love seeing the people on the course and talking with them. I only concentrate when I'm actually shooting. Isn't that strange . . . " her voice trailed off.

"I don't think it's strange at all," I told her. "It doesn't matter at all if you believe you did or did not live the life you just tapped into. What matters is that you pay attention to the information you got and use it now."

We talked after the class. She was still a little amused with what she had experienced.

"I know it's difficult to imagine that it was really you hitting rocks with a stick," I told her. "Don't worry about whether or not you made it up. It seems to me, since you got something so unlike what you had decided would happen, that there is more credibility in the experience. How else can this information help you now?"

"Well, I've been feeling a lot of pressure when I play lately. I feel that everyone is watching me, knowing I'm state champion and that I have to perform everytime I pick up a golf club. It takes some of the fun out of it for me."

"If I were you," I responded, "I would give myself permission to enjoy the game again. Anytime you start feeling that pressure, just take a moment and feel the joy of hitting stones with a stick. Get back in touch with how much fun that was, and why you play golf now. You still have that sense of competition or you wouldn't be state champion, but it's also fun for you. Let it be."

Were these images she had evoked just a clever way for her subconscious to put her back in touch with the fun golf should be for her? Was it permission to excel? And most important, would she use the information to help herself, to be more aware, to enjoy to the utmost a sport that gave her so much pleasure?

Think of a skill or interest you have that comes easily to you. Did you learn quickly, did you amaze others with the ease you displayed in acquiring the skill? It's very possible that this is a clue to another life, another time when that ability had its beginnings.

People have always looked for ways to communicate with their inner selves, to understand their lives. In our technology-oriented society, we have moved far afield from that inner knowledge that was once an integral part of our lives. Remembering your past lives and using that information in the present will bring you closer to the center of yourself, closer to an awareness of the purpose of your life.

Finding Your True Self

I was working in a private session with a woman who was trying to understand why she was blocked in her career. Her skills were highly developed, she had been in business for several years, but still her success was limited. As she came out of hypnosis she said, "Oh, I see, I'm trying to do this as a man would. I'm not a man, I'm me. My way is softer, my way to accomplish my goals must be my own. How the successful men I know have achieved their success has nothing to do with me. I've spent the last seven years trying so hard to emulate successful men, including my ex-husband. He is very good at what he does, as are the other men I've been involved with. They all have this air about them. Although my business is totally unrelated to what any of them do, I still feel the need to be like them so I can be as successful as they are."

"I take it that hasn't worked too well up till now?" I queried.

"No, not at all. No wonder I get so frustrated. I use their yardstick to measure my success. I try to think like them. I must be nuts."

In the regression she had just experienced I had listened to a tale of intrigue, of treasure maps, of deceit. She had been married to and loved the man who had the maps. He had met foul play. None of the people involved were concerned about her—she was "only a woman." And yet she had rescued her husband from the hold of a ship where he was being kept captive. Later he confronted the man who had betrayed him. In the confrontation, her husband had been shot and mortally wounded. She had picked up the gun from the desk where it lay and shot and killed the man who had betrayed and then killed her husband. The only reason she had the opportunity to do this was because she was "only a woman" and not feared by the killer.

As we talked after the session, the ramifications of what she had just experienced continued to amaze her.

"It's so incredibly clear now. I've really been in my own way so much of the time. I need to run my business intuitively. I know what really works for me, what I'm good at. I need to follow sound business strategies, but I really need to pay attention to what makes me and what I do unique. The answer is not in the *Wall Street Journal*. It's in me. I know how to do it, I have the courage, I'm as clever now as I was then—if I didn't just make all that up," she laughed.

"Well, whether you did or not is not the point," I responded. "What you need to take a look at and be aware of is your own uniqueness. They say we choose to be male or female in each life. We choose our circumstances, our opportunities. But it's up to us to use them, to be aware. Maybe this is just your mind's way to make you aware of what you've been doing wrong in the past, and what you can do now to be successful. Can you apply this information to your life now? Will it be helpful? That's really the key here, to give ourselves permission to use what comes from our own minds, to make it work for us."

Do you sometimes feel that you are standing before a door that leads to your success, and for some reason you are not able to reach out and turn the handle? The door remains closed, you stay frustrated, and wonder why. Could there be a clue in your own mind to this behavior? Could a past life give you the key?

In all the years I've done regressions, I have never heard the same story twice. The human mind is so fertile, that it doesn't surprise me. Often when I'm working with private clients and listening to their stories, I get really involved and start thinking to myself, "I bet I know what happened and why they have this conflict." And then as I regress them and the story unfolds, it is never even slightly what I expected. I couldn't possibly have an answer to their dilemma. The key always lies within their own minds, if only they will trust what is offered.

CHAPTER 4

The Past Can Help You Understand

Often when we are having difficulty in our lives, in a relationship, with our job or with our children, we rack our brain for solutions. We overlook the possibility that a past life connection with the area we are working on may give us the needed insight to understand and deal effectively with the current life situation.

Grief and Healing

"I think I understand now. It's still hard to accept, but I think I understand."

The man uttering those words had just explored a lifetime in which he had committed suicide. He had learned self-hypnosis in the past, and now had felt the need to experience a regression to help him deal with a very painful situation in his life. Just weeks prior to our session his best friend had taken his own life. He was overwhelmed with grief, trying so hard to understand why someone he loved so much would choose to end his life.

"If only he had talked with me, had let me know how hopeless he felt. Maybe I could have helped," he told me. "I just can't understand why someone would consider suicide as an option. There's always something we can do about the situations in our lives. To just give up is beyond me."

And yet in the regression he had just experienced, he had reached a point in that other life where taking his own life seemed to be the only answer for him.

I had instructed him to seek out the lifetime that would help him understand his friend's decision and to explore the lifetime that would help him in the grieving process. In the regression he found himself in Germany during World War II. He was an SS officer. When the war ended he was so disheartened with all he had experienced that he made the decision to end his own life. He stood on a bridge to make his decision and then simply jumped.

He was more peaceful after the session. It was as though a great weight had been lifted from his shoulders. The hardest part of dealing with his loss had been his lack of understanding of how anyone could just give up. Finding himself in that place gave him the ability to empathize with his friend's decision. He was now free to grieve and allow himself to heal.

Fantasy? Imagination? Who knows. Once again, the important thing was the release he felt, the lessening of his pain. Perhaps when we are faced with a painful situation in our life, it is because in another time we have been faced with this same situation and through our own or a loved one's experience, we will be given the opportunity to learn, to forgive, to grow.

If understanding a love relationship is your motivation to explore past lives, you can discover the possible past-life tie to any difficulty in the present. You can release the negative influence from that past life and heal the present. It is almost magical to observe someone discover a reason for their present feelings. Once the discovery has been made, that person is able to move on. I have no idea how or why this works, it simply does. In my mind, knowledge is always power, and having knowledge of where or how a situation or feeling began gives us the power to understand, and with our understanding, to move on.

Comfort for a Troubled Relationship

"I'm so happy to know we had a life that was filled with such joy. I was afraid that every time we were together there was pain and separation. I feel better just knowing we were so much a part of each other's lives. There was daily give and take, communication and such deep love."

The woman bubbling with this joy had just experienced a regression taking her to a past life with the same married man she is involved with now. When she came to me, she was angry with herself for accepting so little and wanted to take a hard look at her own needs and get on with her life. In the life she had just explored, she found herself married to this man. They were American Indians living in close harmony with the land, filled with ancient knowledge which they used in their lives. He was a shaman, a medicine man, a healer. During the course of that lifetime she would often go to the top of a hill and stretch her arms to the sky thanking the Great Spirit for the joy and beauty in her life.

"I could actually feel the soft buckskin dress I was wearing," she said. "It was the most spiritual feeling I've ever had. Such a sense of oneness with all of nature, with God, or the Great Spirit, as I knew that power then."

At the end of the regression, when I asked her to be aware of the purpose of that lifetime, she said, "I am to know there are hoops of perfection above me at all times, and when I feel the need I must pause and see them in my mind's eye. I must bring them down and circle my entire being with them, with their peace, their perfection. I am to stay aware of this perfection that is always available to me throughout my life. I am to stay in touch with that joy, that love. It is always there, throughout time. It has no beginning and no end, just as a circle has no beginning and no end."

I listened with rapt attention as she spoke. Her face glowed with an inner peace that had not been evident before our session. She had told me the story of her involvement over many years with this man in the present. Her hunger to be with him was never satisfied. His love for her not enough for him to choose to be with her. The pain in her eyes as she spoke of the long years of wanting what she could not have was now replaced with a look of acceptance.

"Now, no matter what happens, if I choose to stop being involved with him, I will have this memory to call on to offer me solace through a difficult time," she said. "Nothing makes what has been happening easier or takes away the pain, but at least now I know there has been more, and will be again in another time."

Was this just a rationalization for a part of her life with which she was not in accord? Did she need to re-experience their love when they had been together so that she could release him and allow someone else in her life? Would this experience serve as a healing process in her life?

If you are divorced or ending a relationship, finding out about past lives can provide a positive, nurturing avenue to understand how and why you are in these circumstances. You can use this tool to help heal the wounds of divorce, to forgive yourself for your role in the dissolution of the relationship. You can be comfortable with caring and loving again, first yourself, and then another.

Perhaps what we have come here to learn can be learned in the context of a relationship. Our emphasis may be to learn about ourselves within the framework of a relationship. Knowing how the past is affecting us in the present may not change the relationship. It's a good possibility that you need to change, and the challenge in the situation is for you to see the opportunity a particular set of circumstances has given you to grow as a caring, loving person. We can take the wisdom and knowledge gained from that other time into our present life. We can choose to totally release negativity and limitations.

Release from Fear

"Oh how awful, how futile." The woman uttering these words had asked me to direct her to a previous lifetime with her husband. She wanted to explore and understand the seemingly unexplainable feelings she was having about their marriage.

She had been married for fourteen years. Theirs had been a reasonably comfortable marriage, but lately her yearnings for something more had changed the complexion of their relationship. She had returned to college and was working on her master's degree in counseling. Her husband was having trouble with her new-found independence, her need to have goals that did not include him.

The lifetime she had tapped into had taken her back to the time of the wild west. She was an Indian, he a trapper. She had been taken by him as his woman. She had hated him and her captivity. She had run away from him continually, and he had always tracked her down and brought her back. She refused to accept his cruelty and the restrictions in her life. The last time she ran away, he tracked her down and beat her to death in an old deserted cabin.

I had listened in horror to what unfolded as a brutal, heartless story. When the session ended, I thought, "That's the end of that marriage." She had disclosed to me before the session that she had been frightened of her husband lately, fearing he might hurt her.

"Has he ever been physically violent with you?"

"No, he's never hit me. It's not something I would expect of him, but lately I feel afraid. It's a strange feeling, especially since I can't explain it."

Her brow furrowed as she considered what the regression had revealed. She was pensive trying to use this information to gain insight into the direction she needed to take. I was fearful for her.

When I talked with her four months later, she happily reported that the regression had seemed to smooth things out and had given her lots of information about their situation.

"I stopped being afraid after the regression," she said. "It seemed to release that fear I was feeling." When we talked again two years later, her marriage had ended. There had been no violence, but her husband had continued to resist her need to finish her degree and go to work. He wanted her home even though their two boys were older and did not need her to be constantly at home. She had tried to make him understand her need for something more, but he grew more withdrawn and angry as the days passed. The anger was often unexpressed, just a current that ran through their lives. She had sought counseling and had worked on balancing her needs with his, but to no avail.

When we talked she was excited. Life was opening up for her. There were some difficulties, but her life was her own now.

Was what she experienced in a regression a key? Was its purpose to guide her through a troubled time, to help her find herself, to encourage her to have her independence? Was the past teaching her?

If you are experiencing a block in your career, in any endeavor, a past life could very possibly reveal the reason you are stuck at the moment. If you feel like you're up against terrible odds it may be because in several past lives you faced great obstacles. Possibly in that other time you did not use the resources available to you, and this life is an opportunity to be more decisive, to learn and do better. Maybe the creative spark you need to propel you toward success lies within you, and needs only to be recognized to be used.

Past-life regression is an opportunity to learn about aspects of yourself that are applicable to your present search for self-knowledge and improvement. Your own soul history repeats itself until you allow the events (past, present and future) to hold up a mirror for you to see yourself in. Exploring other lives makes you aware of your connection to the universe. You have brought all of your past talents, interests, and loves to this life. How much better to live with that awareness and incorporate that knowledge into your life now. All that you come to understand and use in your life becomes a worthy preparation for your next life. So often we spend our time fixing our attention on our problems and not exploring possible solutions. Past life recall can help you be aware of how very resourceful you have been in the past, and how, once again, you can solve problems creatively in the present.

Recalling past lives provides an opportunity not to live on the surface of life, but to go deeper into self-understanding. It is a way to reinforce and discover your special uniqueness, knowing that death is not the final answer.

CHAPTER 5

Clues to Your Past Lives

Watch Your Dreams

It was a dream that had been repeated over a twenty-five year time span. The man relating his dream to me had never been to the South. He had been born and raised in Oklahoma, and yet this dream had taken him time and again through the events on July 2, 1863, the second day of the Battle of Gettysburg. He was a Confederate soldier in Gen. Hood's brigade. The battle occurred in a peach orchard. Over and over in the dream through the years, he saw Union soldiers carrying rifles and charging. He would vividly see an officer on a horse with his sabre drawn. At that point the dream would become foggy. He relived this scene in his dreams regularly. Over and over it would become foggy at the same point. And then on July 2, 1987, he experienced a terrible day. He felt bad, emotionally and physically. Everything went wrong. Four separate times he was in near-miss auto accidents, far too close for comfort. These were strange near-misses: drivers would pull across four lanes of traffic, as though aiming for his car. All disasters were averted, and at the end of that long day, sitting quietly in the safety of his home, he suddenly became aware that it was the anniversary of the second day of the Battle of Gettysburg, the day he had relived so many times in his dreams.

The dreams ceased. Something within his own subconscious had released him from the horror of that day. It was all over, he could feel it. An interesting note about this man is that in this life he has a hiatial hernia that is about one inch long and one-quarter inch wide—about the size of a sabre wound. Was this another case of conjured memory? A dream to explain a current physical problem? A past life?

Dreams are a way for our subconscious to communicate with us, to call our attention to areas that need our attention. Have you ever dreamed of yourself dressed from another time and place, perhaps not even looking like yourself, and yet knowing it was you? It's a very strong possibility that when we dream of other times and places we are reliving another life. Watch your dreams—they are important clues to past lives.

Instant Recognition of a Place

There are times when a past-life memory is so strong that a visit to the place where the past life occurred is not even necessary. A businessman had come to me for help in using hypnosis to sharpen his skills on the tennis court. Because he knew I also worked with past-life regressions, he told me during our last session of a startling experience he had.

"I was reading a magazine, just quietly relaxing one evening," he said. "I turned the page and there was a full-page color photo of a castle in Europe. I was transfixed by the photograph. The room I was sitting in just faded from my awareness. I was somehow in that picture. I knew what it looked like inside the castle. I just knew. I don't know how, but I knew that I had been there. I knew something important had happened to me in that castle. I can't explain all the feelings I had at the time; I only know how strong they were."

"I think it would be really interesting to explore that place. Let's set up an appointment for you to do just that."

I knew from the experience he described, that as he sat quietly reading a magazine, relaxing at the end of the day, he had drifted into a light altered state of consciousness. When he turned the page of the magazine, because of his relaxed state, his subconscious had surfaced that information for him. It was a lifetime his mind wanted him to be aware of. It was an opportunity to learn more about himself. How interesting that shortly after his experience he ended up in a hypnotist's office to work on his tennis game. Coincidence? Luck? Opportunity?

The following week he came in for his appointment, and yes, he had lived in that place. He knew he had been there, he just didn't know the cast of characters and the issues involved until he explored the life in a regression. During the regression we found that he constantly had to choose between caring for the people he loved and his duty to his country. He had spent many hours walking on the hills surrounding the castle reflecting on choices he had to make.

As we talked after the regression he was reflective once again, telling me of the choices he had made in his present life involving his family. He opted several times to forego business opportunities that would have taken away from the close relationship he had with his wife and son in the present. The decisions so painfully made in that other time had been strengthened in the present. He became aware that the allegiance begun centuries before were continuing to be fulfilled in his life now. The love experienced so long ago had deepened with the passing of time.

Often clients tell me about a family vacation, a time when they were touring historic places. They may be walking through a New England town, a city in Europe, or a beach in Hawaii, and suddenly be overwhelmed with feelings of sadness, or great joy, or just a sense that they have been there before.

So often we receive clues from our minds about past lives, and just as often we don't understand the feelings, or simply choose to ignore what we experience.

Instant Recognition of a Person

We all have occasions when we meet someone and immediately experience strong feelings of comfort and deep communication. Barbara wanted to explore a past-life connection with a woman she had met by chance several months before. She had attended a lecture at the library. All through the talk she had the feeling that she had met the speaker before. When the lecture ended, she approached the woman and said, "I feel we've met sometime in the past, I really feel like I know you."

"I know," the other woman replied. "I've been watching you throughout my talk, and I have the same feeling."

They stood for the next fifteen minutes going over the places they had both lived for the past twenty years, trying to discover where and how they had met. They spoke of possible mutual friends, mutual interests, anything that would give them a clue to this overwhelming feeling they were both experiencing. Nothing came to the fore. They both left the meeting puzzled over this strange experience. Before they parted they made a lunch date for the following week. They both felt strongly about not losing contact with each other.

At their luncheon the next week, sitting in a busy restaurant, they talked openly of their lives. They spoke of their fears, their dreams, and aspirations. There was none of the facade that we normally wear with new acquaintenances. They were just two people sharing their inner selves with each other. They both knew at the end of their three-hour lunch that they had formed a friendship that would always be part of their lives. Barbara was curious to know why this new friendhip had been so swift and deep. In her regression she went to a time when she and her new friend had been sisters. Because of the death of their parents the sisters had been separated. After the regression she was aware of why her new friendship felt so important. She also could explain her feelings about maintaining contact with her friend.

Unexplained Fears

"I need to talk with you in person about a fear I have that I would like to explore in a regression," the woman said when making an appointment.

"Yes, we'll take all the time you need before we do the session," I answered. I thought to myself, "This must be very important to her. She's not even willing to talk about it on the phone."

When she arrived for her appointment the following week, her need to talk about what she was feeling became very apparent. She leaned forward in her chair, watching my face, needing me to understand how strongly she felt about the regression she wanted to do. She explained she had four children, all grown now and on their own. Her face glowed as she spoke of each of them, proud as only a parent can be. However, she had always been fearful about one of her daughters. This daughter was now grown and had a good marriage and children of her own, all that a mother could want for her child. And yet this fear continued to haunt her life.

"When the children were growing up," she explained, "I had the usual concern I think all parents do about their children. But what I felt about her was unusual and not based on anything that had happened to her. She, like all my kids, had the usual cuts, scrapes, and bruises. Nothing ever happened to her that required more than two stitches. Even now it's as though I wait for something awful to happen, dreading that it will. My intuition tells me that there must be a past life connection here, something carried over that I need to be aware of so I can release this fear. When the kids were little I used to lie in bed at night and think things like, 'If the house burns, how will I get her out of the house?' Of course I was concerned about all the kids, but I always focused on how I would save her in the event of some disaster. Nothing ever happened that required me to act on those fears, but they continue. I would really like to work this out and be done with it."

I listened carefully to all she said. As a mother, I could certainly understand what she was talking about, but I couldn't identify with a fear that overwhelming.

"What is your daughter's name?" I asked.

"Carole," she said. "This is so strange, I feel foolish even disclosing all this to you."

"Don't worry, I've heard much stranger, believe me."

We then explored the lifetime that would give her insight into the feelings she had harbored for so many years. She went to a lifetime when Carole, her daughter, had been her wife. She had been male in that other time and had been in love with this beautiful woman. They lived in the Deep South on a plantation. They had wealth and position, but all of their advantages could not save them from tragedy. The first year of their marriage a child had been conceived. They were elated at the prospect of this new joy in their life, but both wife and child died in childbirth. The grief felt by my client was beyond imagination. He blamed himself for his wife's death and hated himself for being party to it. He grieved and grieved, turning from everyone who loved him and wanted to console him. Consumed with pain, he struck out with rage at helpless slaves. He died several years later, never accepting the blow fate had dealt him.

Now, several hundred years later, those painful scars were still part of this woman's consciousness. By knowing where those feelings about her child in this life had come from, she was finally in control of her feelings. She could finally accept and release what had happened in another time. I spent considerable time at the end of the regression instructing her to release at conscious and subconscious levels all negativity from that previous experience. I took her into the highest levels of her mind and asked her the lesson learned in that time.

"To trust, to love, to be unafraid."

Grief that had been pent up for centuries was released and healed. She could now enjoy her daughter without constant fear.

Past-Life Talents That Are With You Now

So often talents we possess are skills that have been developed in another time. Each of us has unique abilities. Past lives can also provide us with clues to skills that could be easily relearned in the present.

Using Your Talents

"I need help with the block I have in my writing," the pleasant young man in my office said. "I've known for years that I really needed to write, that it was very important to me at many different levels, but I continue to avoid sitting down and writing."

"Writing is a lonely business, it's something no one can do for you or with you. It requires tremendous self-discipline," I responded. "Since I write, I'm familiar with what you're telling me. Tell me about your writing. When did you begin? How long have you wanted to write?"

"Since I was a small child, I've recorded important events in my life in written form. I've been compelled to write, to put my thoughts on paper. I enjoy the process of writing, of seeing the words appear, of feeling that I've expressed myself."

I could see the feelings he expressed in his eyes. They were the eyes of a poet, of a very sensitive person. He obviously felt very strongly about wanting to know more about a past life that would help him be more effective in the present. He told me that he was divorced. He and his ex-wife had remained good friends but had simply been unable to live together. As we talked further, the reason for his divorce became evident. His writing made her feel excluded from his world. She felt she couldn't compete with his interest in and need to write. She resented the time he spent plying his craft.

"It will be interesting to explore past life connections to the block you're experiencing," I said. "Let's see what the past can tell us about your desire to write."

When we began the session he first went to a scene in his current life, one that had great meaning to him. It was a time of contentment and inner peace with his former wife. I continued moving him back in time, determined that we would discover the past life tie to the block to his creativity. As so often happens in a first regression, each time I moved him in time he would tap into a different lifetime. We explored three different lives, all of which affected his writing. In one he was the publisher of a newspaper and wrote profusely. His wife in that life had insisted he get rid of the paper and devote more time to his family. He had done what she requested and spent the remainder of that life feeling unfulfilled because the work he so loved was no longer part of his life.

And then he found himself in Pompeii, in the midst of pandemonium, as the mountain erupted. Surviving the destruction that enveloped the city, he knew that it was important for him to record all that had happened, especially his feelings of fear and confusion.

And then, as the clock ticked away only minutes in the present, we spun to another life that would help him understand the present. With my next suggestion he found himself talking with an older man, someone he described as being very wise. He told me this man was his mentor, someone who encouraged him and taught him. He felt the person was a very important philosopher in his time, possibly even Socrates.

I continued asking him to move to another significant event, to a time when what occurred would give him insight into his life. His mentor and he spent hours talking of life and its meaning. He found himself feeling very skeptical when this wise old man spoke of an ancient civilization called Atlantis. His mentor talked of great wisdom and knowledge from that time and wanted him to write of that other time. He wanted him to be aware that he had been part of that ancient civilization.

"What did you do If you didn't believe this place existed, how could you write about it?"

"I moved beyond my doubt. I began to remember the things we talked of and it became very real to me. It was something I had experienced. For some reason it was important for me to record my memories."

As he talked I felt my own mind racing to Shirley MacLaine's book, *It's All in the Playing*. There were several pages I thought he should read. I felt strongly they would evoke memories from him of time he had spent in Atlantis. The part of the book my mind raced to was her experience in Peru at the Inca ruin called Ollantaitambo. She had "remembered" being in this place, and as she climbed to an ancient temple memories of that other time had become part of her conscious awareness. Somehow I knew that the young man reclining in the chair in my office would write about Atlantis and about the things Shirley MacLaine had recalled in that ancient ruin. It was an exhilitating experience for me, to be so certain that he would read those pages and understand them.

As we concluded the regression, I guided him into the highest levels of his mind to seek the lesson to be learned from the lives he had just explored.

His words gave tremendous clues to the blocks he had been experiencing and insight into how to conduct his life. "I was meant to write, no matter what, and to persist. It was important that I tell the truth as I saw it."

When I asked about the purpose of his life in Pompeii he said, "In so many of my lives I've compromised. Because I was fearful I never did what I really wanted to do."

When I asked him to be aware of the lesson learned in the life he experienced as the publisher of a newspaper, his words were true for all of us and very important for him; "Happiness comes from doing what you love to do. I needed to listen to my own instincts and have persistence, dedication, and a high standard of ethics. I must be true to myself."

As he opened his eyes I could see the look of disbelief on his face. He was shaking his head, obviously trying to assimilate all he had experienced. "I can't believe all of that came from me. I wonder if I made some of it up—or all of it?"

"I don't think so," I said. "Think about your life now, your compelling desire to write, how thwarted you feel when you don't write. Look at what happened in those other lives when you were not true to yourself. Obviously your subconscious is trying very hard to tell you what you need to be doing. Now you need to to listen, to understand, and to use this information. Trust yourself."

I then began to tell him of my thoughts while he was in hypnosis about Shirley MacLaine's book and the pages I felt so strongly he should read. I told him I would call later that evening and read the pages to him. I told him I felt these particular pages would ring a bell for him, would evoke memories of his own time in Atlantis, and would probably compel him to write, once again, of his experiences from that time.

"Curious you should be talking about my writing about Atlantis," he said. "Just two evenings ago I spent considerable time thinking of just that, writing about Atlantis."

"Bingo," I said. "I'll talk with you later this evening and read those pages to you."

When we next talked I read him the pages from *It's All in the Playing*. He was silent until I finished, and then he told me he felt he had been there himself, knew the words I read before I even spoke them.

Was this fact or fantasy? Do we need to spend time concerning ourselves with the existence of Atlantis? Could this young man actually have known Socrates? Would he choose to ignore this information, once again being untrue to himself? Or would this experience unleash his creativity and motivate him to write about his thoughts and feelings? That in my mind was the only issue.

Over and over in the regressions I conducted compelling information surfaced about talents and abilities people possessed and needed to use. Again and again I saw people breaking through to a sense of personal power.

Déjà Vu Experiences

Most of us have experienced a feeling of *déjà vu*, that eerie feeling that makes the hair stand up on the back of your neck. Because of the nature of my work, people often tell me of these experiences. Often they are so curious they decide to explore further in a regression. Others have no need to explore with a past life regression because the experience was so complete that no questions were left unanswered.

Robert told me of his experience in Hawaii. His trip had been long planned. He had anticipated going to Hawaii with excitement, collecting travel brochures for months before the trip. Once in Hawaii, he enjoyed every minute—the beaches, the sunsets, the lush tropical setting were all idyllic. Two days before he was to return to the mainland, he and a friend decided to climb to the top of a nearby mountain to watch the sun rise. They carefully made their way up a narrow path, realizing they should have brought a flashlight to see where they were walking. They proceeded, anxious to be at the top before dawn. Robert said as he walked the ground beneath his feet began to feel familiar. He could feel many others walking with him up this mountain. It was as though he had walked this path many times in a ritualistic way, with purpose. Suddenly his feelings changed and he stopped abruptly, putting out his hand to stop his friend. He knew they should not proceed another step. He sensed danger. His friend thought he was being a little strange, but Robert was so adamant his friend decided it would be foolish to argue. They stood for perhaps fifteen minutes waiting for the first rays from the sun to touch their path. As the day dawned, both were amazed to see that their path abruptly ended only a few feet in front of them. A cliff was directly in front of them. Had they proceeded further, they would have fallen to certain death.

Robert had never been to Hawaii and had certainly never walked this path before. Yet he knew that danger lay just ahead. A horrible accident was avoided because he paid attention to his instincts, to that part of his mind that is so available, but so often ignored.

Gail told me of an experience in Scotland. Her trip was one that she had dreamed of for years. An unexpected windfall of funds had made the trip possible. As she eagerly toured castles, one made a lasting impression. A former dungeon had been converted into an elegant dining room. As she entered the dungeon, she was overwhelmed with feelings she couldn't explain. Despite the gleaming crystal, linen table-cloths, and flowers, Gail felt terror spread through her body. She felt a need to have her back against a wall. Her instinct was to slide to the floor, doubled over to protect herself from blows from an unknown source. Tears welled up in her eyes. She knew she had experienced some sort of horror in that place. The chains and manacles still hung from the walls, an ominous reminder of a former time. She quickly left the room, knowing that she would probably embarrass herself in front of the others on the tour if she didn't get out of there immediately.

Had she actually been imprisoned in that place, or a similar one? Had she been chained to a wall and beaten? Where did that rush of emotion come from? It was certainly not part of the present environment in the room. Did she tap into the energy of those who had suffered in that place? Were the very walls so imbued with those feelings that she, being a sensitive person, had felt the horror of time past?

Carole told me of her experience in a large convention center. Friends invited her to hear a priest speak. They told her many who attended experienced his special abilities to heal. Carole is not Catholic, but she is always open to learning and experiencing new things. The presentation lasted well over two hours. Carole noted many who responded to the healing energy the priest obviously possessed. She witnessed several who felt they had been personally touched or blessed through him. To celebrate the closing of the service, the priest stepped from the stage, adorned in the vestments of his faith and carrying before him a tall cross. As he moved slowly through the crowd and circled the entire auditorium, he disappeared in the crowd. At that point the room and energy changed for her. She was transported back to the time of Christ. She "knew" that once she had witnessed Christ moving through a crowd. The incredible power and beauty of the experience was overwhelming. Tears flowed down her cheeks. She could hear celestial music. She knew beyond a shadow of a doubt that once, long ago, she had experienced this wonder. It was as though two moments in time, one almost two thousand years before and one in the present, had touched and melded into one.

Had she been in the presence of Christ long ago? Were these stirrings from deep within her part of her innate spirituality? Was this event to remind her of her divinity? Years have passed since this experience, but it is burned into her mind forever, as one of those life-changing events that bring an awareness that we are more than our physical bodies.

Think about déjà vu experiences you have had. What were your feelings? Did you get more information later, or were the moments you had the experience all there was?

Déjà vu experiences are certain clues to other lives. They are an indication to you that something of great importance happened to you in that other time. It is probably something your subconscious wants you to be aware of, or there would have been no recall. These moments are an interesting facet of the mind to explore.

CHAPTER 6

How Can I Begin to Remember My Past Lives?

The easiest, most gentle way to begin to allow yourself to remember your past lives is by taking a look at the things around you as possible clues to other times. Think, for instance, of the furnishings in your home, the style of clothing you prefer for work and for relaxation. Do you have antiques in your home? Are there special family heirlooms or treasures you hold dear? A quilt your grandmother or great-grandmother made, an old bureau, a sugar spoon? How do you feel when you look at those things, or touch them? Perhaps these antiques evoke feelings because you lived in the time they were created.

Do you like to dine by candlelight? Does the soft glow of candles create special feelings within you? Could it be that you have shared many meals with those you love in another life? Does that glow evoke buried memories?

Are you drawn to a certain period in history? Have you traveled to Europe or to historic places in America and found yourself experiencing feelings that went beyond the explanations of your tour guide? If you could travel anywhere in the world and spend three months, what place would you choose?

Were you born in the city, love visiting farms or driving in the countryside? Do you love to garden, and even in the city have you taken a corner of your patio to grow vegetables? Is your house filled with lush, tropical plants? Do things grow easily for you? Perhaps you have an innate sense of how to grow things, knowledge garnered from another time.

Are you a lover of books? Do you often browse in bookstores for relaxation? Are you filled with curiosity about many things, always studying and learning something new? How do you feel when you walk on the campus of a university? Think for a moment about the kinds of things you read for leisure: could they possibly be a clue to past lives? Could you have been a scholar in another place and time?

What about writing? Do you write in your career? Do you dream of writing the great American novel? Is it a pleasure for you to express yourself with the written word? Do you write long, thoughtful letters to friends rather than pick up the phone? Could any of these things be an indication of abilities acquired in another time?

What kind of work do you do? Is it highly technical? Are your skills with people highly developed? Do friends tend to tell you their deepest feelings? Do you enjoy being in large groups of people, or do you prefer intimate gatherings of just a few friends? Reflect for a few moments about your work and the skills you use. Is it possible that once, long ago, you developed these skills for other purposes?

Were you a child who took everything apart? Do you like to build things, to invent? Have you ever thought up a device you seriously considered patenting? It's a possibility you were a scientist or inventor in another time.

What are your hobbies? Do you like to work with wood, sail a boat, collect seashells or stamps, pewter, crystal? How do you feel when you are involved in your hobby or interest? Do you find contentment and inner peace? What do you suppose your connection to these activities might be, if you set your imagination free? Might it tie you to a past life?

Do you look at the stars and wonder about what's out there, what is the pattern and rhythm to the heavens? Have you bought or wanted a telescope to study the stars? Have you joined an astronomy club? Perhaps you once were part of a place like Stonehenge, which is aligned to the stars.

How do you spend weekends and holidays? Do you like to go camping, white-water canoeing, hiking, fishing, hunting? Maybe you enjoy just being outdoors, walking in a park or in the woods. These activities can give insight into past lives.

What kind of music do you most love to listen to? Do you play an instrument? If you studied music, was there a composer whose music was easy for you to learn? When you play the instrument you have studied, do you become lost in the music, losing track of time? Could this be a clue to an ability that had its beginnings in another life?

Have you noticed that each person in your family is an individual, with particular likes and dislikes, habits and idiosyncrasies? Even though each child in the family was raised by the same parents, in the same household, differences are very obvious. Where do these personal preferences come from? Could it possibly be that you were all part of other families in the past, and have come together now, weaving your lives together, learning from each other?

Do you have a fear of water or heights? Is there any phobia or fear you have that you cannot connect to any occurence in your life? Very often these unexplained phobias or fears are connected to an event from a past life.

Have you ever gone to a psychic for a reading? Do you know your birth sign and the characteristics attributed to that particular sign? Have you ever studied numerology, astrology, or taken a class in developing your intuition? Is reincarnation a subject that has interested you, even though it is not part of your family's belief system? Long ago studies of this sort were common and used by people for information in their lives. Your interest today may reflect your daily use of these systems in another time.

More important than places and things are relationships. Often the significant people in our lives are people we have been involved with before. If we view our lives as a school-house, an opportunity to learn about ourselves and to learn to love, then the people in our lives are incredibly important. We seem to come back and choose much the same cast of characters from the past. So often I am asked, "Do you mean that I was married to my husband/wife before?" My answer is almost always in the affirmative, since from the hundreds of regressions I've done certain patterns emerge. The pattern is that we have lessons to learn, things to work out. Since we don't live in a vacuun, the people in our lives provide us with the opportunity to grow as individuals. Each person in our life, whether lover, friend, or enemy, is an opportunity for us to understand our own lessons.

Take a few moments and think about the people in your life. How did you meet your wife/husband? Was there an instant recognition when you were introduced? Did you become fond of each other over a period of time? Think for a few moments of your parents, brothers, sisters, aunts, uncles, cousins. Has any of them created a great impact on your life? Did you have a favorite teacher in school, a neighbor who spent time teaching you how to play ball or crochet? Any and all of these people can give you clues to your past lives.

It is interesting to watch a group of people work with this material. They begin talking about the things they've collected over the years, seashells, samurai swords, antique locks. All of a sudden they begin to examine their lives a little more closely, to wonder about the people and things in their life, the travels they have done, the strong feelings evoked with no apparent cause. It is also an opportunity to understand those we love a little more. Consider the telescope your children had to have, the camping trips, the collection of antique dolls, the multitude of books read and subjects studied: are these reflection of times past that are important in the present?

I don't believe that we are living in a harsh, cruel system of an "eye for an eye and a tooth for a tooth." If I was unkind to someone in a past life, that doesn't mean that in this life I must allow them to harm me. If we have chosen to be together again, it is an opportunity to work out past conflicts, to go beyond the difficulties we encountered in the past. A belief in reincarnation does not give us license to treat people unkindly, to create pain in another's life. Believing you have lived before and are now living a life chosen by yourself because of its unique opportunities makes you accountable for your attitudes, actions, and reactions. It removes your ability to blame others for your situation. It is truly a way to grow at all levels.

Spend some time now with pen and paper in hand to do some detective work that will give you clues to some of your past lives.

Exercise: Identifying Clues to Your Past Lives

1. Make a list of your favorite kinds of furniture. Do you own antiques, or want to own them? From what historical time and place?
2. What is your favorite ethnic food?
3. Write down all the places you have been to, or have seen in photographs, that really touched you.
4. List your hobbies and interests and the feelings you have when you are involved in them.
5. Make a list of the skills that were easy for you to learn. They can be work- or leisure-related.
6. What historical period most interests you? Are you fascinated by the Civil War, the building of the pyramids, or how the West was won?

7. Write about collections you have had at any time in your life. How did you become interested in that particular collection?

8. List the people in your family who have most affected your life. How do you feel about them, how did they feel about you?

9. List close friends, neighbors, teachers who have had an effect on your life.

By completing the above exercise you have given yourself an opportunity to take a look at some strong clues to other lives. Now take your list and decide which area you would like to explore. Close your eyes for a few moments and think about what you have written. If it is about a place, how do you feel when you think of that particular place? What do you remember the most, what about that place had the strongest effect on you? Write down everything you feel.

Developing Right-Brain Awareness

Scientists have discovered that the left side of the brain generally performs analytical and verbal functions, while the right side handles spatial and visual functions, intuition, and holistic perception. Because of the values in our society, most of us favor the left side, but the right side can be developed, opening up an exciting new world of perception.

The following exercises are, for the moment, trips into fantasy. They are a way for you to get in touch with the free-flowing, right-brain part of yourself. Allow yourself to trust whatever story you choose to make up. If ten people did the same exercise and allowed themselves to create a fantasy situation, each would come up with a different story. This is a way for you to begin to trust impressions from your mind. Do these exercises at a time of day that is normally spent in a quiet, reflective way.

Exploring a Place

Choose a place you have written about, study your notes, and then expand on them. Write how you felt when you were there, what triggered the feelings, who was with you. Re-create that place in your mind very vividly. Use photographs if you have them available to refresh your memory.

The second step is to sit or lie comfortably, close your eyes, and once again see and feel that place in your mind. Make it as real as it was the day you were there. And then, begin to let your mind drift and float to an imaginary time. Make no judgments about what you see and feel, simply allow your mind free rein. As you begin to see and feel the place again, give yourself this suggestion: "I give myself permission to remember, once again, being there. I will create a story about having been there in a past life."

Have a tape recorder and blank tape ready to record your feelings and thoughts. If you'd prefer, you can write what you experience. Fantasize a time when you were there. Make up any kind of story that pleases you. While you are creating this imaginery time, add all the details you can. How you were dressed, where you lived, how you got your food, the people who lived with you. Write it all down, or record it. Allow it to be as real as the couch or chair you are on, trusting the images and feelings that come to you.

Keep in mind that this is an exercise for yourself. You do not need to share what you write or record with anyone. You are simply exploring possibilities that can lead you to an awareness of other lives and times.

You can do this exercise with each item you have written about. Let your imagination run free. Trust everything that comes to you. This is a journey through your own mind. It will have as much meaning for you as you allow. What you come up with will be unique to you, it will not mean a great deal to anyone else. Here is an example.

A Sample Journal Entry

I can think of and feel the Sierra Nevada mountains so easily. Their majesty and beauty touches me deeply. I feel awe-struck when I look at and stand before the jutting rock formations, the tall pines. I can hear the wind moving through the pines, creating a special music of its own. I feel peaceful there, filled with the wonder of the universe. As I allow my mind to drift I can begin to feel myself there. It is dusk, the sun is setting in a blaze of color. It is a magical time of day, filled with peace and power. I am in a clearing kneeling before a campfire. I am alone. I am a man, an Indian. I can feel the sun touching my body. I have a deep reverence for this place. The day has been fruitful, and tomorrow I will be with my people once again. I stand and raise my arms to the sky, palms outstretched, filling my soul with the beauty of this place. I am thanking the Great Spirit for the bounty of my hunt, for the peace in my life. I stand like this for three or four minutes, feeling a slight breeze gently brushing my skin. I sense a deep commitment to this place, to its sacredness. I feel this is a special place I come to when I need to restore myself. It is a special ritual or ceremony I do to keep myself peaceful within. It is something I do not share with others. It is a special part of me. (The feelings and images that followed were of returning to an encampment with thirty or forty other people and assuming a different persona. What I experienced in the wilderness was very personally mine and was not shared with the others in my camp. It was a deeply religious feeling.)

This person's writing gave her some very definite clues to the feelings she has while in the mountains. She is not a member of any organized church. She experiences her most profound spiritual feelings while in the mountains. Although she has traveled through many different mountain ranges none of them have the particular affect that the Sierra Nevadas do. She also reported that she is deeply private about her spiritual feelings. She was somewhat surprised to see herself as a man, but felt certain she was male in the life she tapped into.

This exercise gave her some important clues about her feelings about life. Obviously, it is very important for her to include being outdoors as part of her daily life to stay tuned to the wonderful feelings she experienced in that clearing in the mountains.

Another woman had been drawn to Vermont. She wondered if her story explained why she loved being there so much. The story she wrote was from the perspective of a young woman who enjoyed gala balls, suitors, and the beautiful farm she and her family lived on. Her father had amassed a fortune in the textile industry, and with that money had bought a "huge farm badly in need of repair. While he was in the process of restoration he fell in love with it. I loved the rolling green mountains and rock walls. There were trees on our hillside. Spring and summer was a riot of color as each week a new plant blossomed. The sound of the streams bouncing and laughing over the rocks gave me peace. The fall was a riot of color—the shades and hues of the leaves expressed all my emotions. I loved this land and knew that soon I would be choosing one of my suitors to marry. I had carefully excluded any who were not as attracted to this area as I."

A geologist described his favorite place as "a large valley surrounded on three sides by forested mountains. It is a special place for me as well as for the animals. I do not cultivate the land, I just live there. I explore the surrounding mountains for the beauty I can find there in the rocks, the trees, the animals, the scenery. The greatest experience this place offers me is nature itself, solitude, and myself. Each day I learn something new about nature and myself. My interest in the place grows and grows because of this. There is no end to the discoveries that exist here. I am accepted by the animals and enjoy a friendship with many of them, large and small. This gives me great satisfaction." Along the side of his paper he wrote, "I sense I have a great knowledge and understanding of this."

Another woman wrote of Scotland. She has not traveled to Scotland, but said, "I am drawn there. I melt when I talk to a man with a Scottish accent. As I allow myself to go back and let the images come, I see that I am a woman in a small village, perhaps just an encampment. I have the feeling that I have been named a witch because of my psychic abilities. A picture comes to my mind that they are pressing my head between boards. This is strange, because as I started to 'make up' a story, it was going to be a love story, but different images came. This is especially interesting to me because in this life I am very intuitive but block those abilities."

As you can see from these examples, the places described evoke many emotions. These feelings are strong clues to a past-life tie with the place described.

Ways of Exploring a Place

If you have a fireplace, build a fire and sit comfortably before it, staring into the flames. People have gathered around fires since time began. It is a common denominator, something that evokes feelings in everyone. Allow yourself to stare into the flames, breathing deeply and calmly, relaxing your body and mind, and then set your mind free. Give yourself the suggestion that you will remember another time you have gazed into the flames of a fire. Allow yourself to recall who was with you, how you felt, where you were. If you don't have a fireplace, you can accomplish the same thing in a public campground.

If you love the ocean, or if you have a favorite stream, go to that place. Make yourself comfortable, close your eyes, hear the lapping of the water, feel the moisture in the air. Concentrate for a time on the sound and feeling of the place you're in, and then allow yourself to drift once again, to remember another time. Begin to fantasize, seeing and feeling yourself in another time. Trust your mind, make up anything that feels good.

Do you like to lie beneath a giant tree and watch the sky through the branches? If so, go outside, lie on the ground, relax your body, hear the wind moving through the tree branches, allow yourself to be there, to feel this place. Then, once again, set your imagination free, give yourself permission to drift back in time, to remember when you have been in a similar place. Do the same thing watching the night sky. The stars have been over our heads in all of our past lives— we have surely studied and wondered at them.

Lie on a large boulder in the sun. Allow the warmth to penetrate into your very being. Feel the sun touching you, the boulder beneath you. After you have relaxed and tuned yourself to the place you have chosen, allow your mind to drift back in time to your connection to this place.

All of these exercises above give you an opportunity to get back in touch with your connection to the earth and the part nature has played in your life, both in this one and in others. Nature is timeless. It has always been a part of our lives and always evokes feelings from deep within us. It provides a wonderful backdrop for buried memories of other times.

Exploring a Relationship

Take time now to think of a very special person in your life, someone you hold near and dear. Close your eyes and relax, think about that person for a few moments. Feel his or her presence, say his or her name in your mind. See his or her eyes. Feel this person looking at you. It is not the color of the eyes that matters, or shape, it is the feeling of that particular person, his or her true nature. Use the eyes of this person to discover a past life.

A Sample Meditation about a Relationship

When I allow myself to focus on Wayne's eyes, I feel protected and loved. I trust him completely, he is a friend, a lover. My feelings change like the turning of a kaleidoscope: different colors, different feelings. As I allow my mind to drift, I can feel us walking together, side by side. It's cold. We seem to have a common purpose. There is something we are doing together that is equally important for both of us. I am wearing a long cloak with a hood. He is dressed in clothing from another time. It is a cold, raw day, the wind is coming from the sea. Fog envelopes us, the dampness penetrates our very bones. We are not speaking, but linked by this common purpose. I feel it is a night that will change our lives. We are standing before a building. There is only one light shining from the windows of the building. We know the man we need to see is within. We climb stairs, I can hear the creaking of the wood, can smell the mustiness of the stairwell. I have a sense of dread, and yet a determination to pursue this person. We are now standing in his office, before a great oak desk. The lamplight is soft, illuminating only the desk. The rest of the room remains in deep shadow. There are shelves filled with books—I can smell the leather of their covers. The man talking with us has betrayed us and put us in jeopardy. We leave the office in anger. The scene fades out at this point.

This example includes definite images and feelings: dampness, fog, a musty smell. The woman who wrote this could allow that drama to continue by simply giving herself instructions to be there again, to allow the story to unfold. When I questioned her, she spoke of a deep friendship with the man she was focusing on. Their lives had been linked and then separated many times over the past twenty years. They were not together in the present, but each knew the other's feelings. There was mutual trust. She told me their friendship often transcended words and the thousands of miles that separated them.

This exercise gave her an opportunity to understand some of the feelings in their relationship and to see a possible past life connection. What she wrote is a good example of the richness of material available from within our own minds.

As we were beginning this exercise one evening in a workshop, a woman in the class said, "I'd like to explore the interest I have in a painting I saw in a gallery in San Francisco."

"That sounds interesting," I responded. "Tell me about the painting. What is in the picture? Do you feel as if you know the people in it?"

"There are people on a Chinese junk sitting in a harbor, I guess in Hong Kong. I just have such strong feelings about it I'd like to explore it. Is that possible?"

"Why not?" was my response. She concentrated on the painting and then wrote:

"There are many of us around the fire. We are sewing small bags of tea into very fine cloth. There are many babies all asleep. We have scarves on our heads and the air is damp. I can hear voices in the background, but we are all silent. I have many teeth missing. My clothes are loose, and my shoes are tight. We are all smoking as we sew. Some people are wearing skin hats and smoking pipes. It is night, and the moon must be full, for it is very bright in the darkness. I see bowls of fish broth being passed and clumps of rice. We are sipping tea and eating rice with our fingers in big clumps. I can feel with my tongue the places where teeth are missing."

"Obviously you once lived on a Chinese junk," I said. It's really amazing that you so easily allowed yourself to walk into the picture."

"What's really strange is the fact that in this life I don't smoke and have never smoked. Also, I have a fetish about taking good care of my teeth. The feeling of the missing teeth was very strong."

Another woman focused on the eyes of her husband. She wrote, "I feel safe, comfortable, able to share most of my thoughts. I also have teasing, angry, confrontive feelings. I feel that he is trying to control me, mold me into a pattern that suits him. It was during the time of knighthood and chivalry. He was a knight and I was his lady. I gave him a pale lavender scarf to carry into battle. He tied it to the silver bridle of his white stallion. It fluttered in the wind as he sat on horseback and bade me farewell. He was going to the crusades. My father was a wealthy nobleman. I was considered of marriageable age and had many suitors seeking to wear my colors. This man attracted me because of his sincerity and intense desire. He would look at me with such longing that it touched my heart and yet at the same time made me afraid of the power he would have over me if I were to love him. He rode off and I wondered if I would ever see him again. The landscape was fairly barren and rocky with a few huge old scraggly trees off to the right."

What she had imagined reflected her life with her husband in the present. There is deep love, interlaced with her need for independence. She told me she spends equal amounts of time supporting him in his endeavors and working on her own personal development and career. Like so many of us, she must learn to love without fear.

Fact or fantasy, it matters not. The only thing that matters is to write about your feelings, looking for ways to better understand a present relationship. Being aware gives you an opportunity to see inside yourself a little more clearly, to understand feelings that transcend the ordinary.

CHAPTER 7

Experiments in Past-Life Recall

If you have had a strong *déjà vu* experience, you can explore it further. When a message comes through so vividly from our subconscious about having experienced something before, it is an indication that it has impact and importance in the present.

Exploring a Déjà Vu Experience

Once again, sit or lie comfortably, close your eyes, breathe deeply, allow yourself to relax. When you have achieved a deep state of relaxation, bring back your *déjà vu* experience. Recreate every detail of what happened when you had the experience. Where were you? Feel the ground beneath your feet, the space around you. What was the temperature, the time of year, the day of the week? Was anyone with you? Were they part of the experience? What triggered the flashback you had? Think of every facet of the experience. Then go back in your mind: sense, see, and feel everything very clearly. Once you have mentally reviewed your experience in detail, give yourself these instructions: "I will allow my *déjà vu* experience to expand, I will receive more details, more insight." You may need to repeat this several times, and then trust yourself as you travel back in time. It may take several attempts before you unlock the door to your subconscious. Be persistent.

Have paper and pen ready to record what you receive. If you would prefer, you can talk into a tape recorder. Record what comes to you in whatever way is most comfortable for you.

You can also ask your subconscious to give you additional information in a dream. Suggest to yourself as you are drifting off to sleep, "I will have a dream tonight about my *déjà vu* experience. It will be very vivid. I will remember absolutely every detail. This will be the last dream I have before I awaken in the morning. I want more information." To indicate to your subconscious that you are serious about wanting more information, place a pen and paper beside your bed to write your dream down immediately upon awakening.

Experiment: Faces Over a Candle

This is an interesting experiment to do with a friend. It is another exercise to help you get in touch with the creative part of your brain. It is an experiment to unlock the door to your subconscious.

You will need a candle in a candle holder. Place the candle on a table between yourself and the person you are going to explore with. Turn all the lights off and sit facing each other. The candle flame should be just below eye level. Begin by relaxing completely, doing some deep breathing to help yourself relax. When you feel relaxed, gaze directly into each other's eyes. As you do so, the face of the person you are looking at will begin to change to other faces. You will be seeing your friend as you have known him or her in other lives. You can talk with each other while you are doing this, describing out loud what you are seeing. Be aware of the thoughts that come to your mind. Do you associate the face you're seeing with any particular time in history? Is it familiar in some way to you? What was your relationship in the previous life?

Do this for a few minutes, and then before what you see leaves your conscious awareness, make notes. If there was a particular face that was compelling, that you were really fascinated with, use that face as a focal point for further exploration. To do so, once again sit or lie comfortably, take some slow deep breaths, and allow your mind to drift back to that face. Give yourself the following instructions: "I will go back to a life connected to the face I saw. I give myself permission to create a story that goes with that face and the feelings I had when the face was before me. Vivid impressions will come to my mind. I trust myself completely."

Questions to Ask a Child

Children have past life recall when they are very young, before they are told by our society that such things do not exist. If you have a small child, up to about four or five years old, you can ask the child a question about his or her past life tie with you. The answer may amaze you.

One of my clients explored a life in which her daughter had been her child in a past life. Her husband had also been with her and the child in that time. In the other lifetime the child was killed in an automobile accident. My client had not discussed her regression with either her husband or her child. In conversation I mentioned to her that she could ask her little girl why she had chosen her for a mother in this life. When asked, the little girl, totally unaware of her mother's experience, replied, "Oh, because you lost me that time, remember?"

When this exchange took place my client and her child were driving to the grocery store. My client reported she was so startled, she could hardly believe her ears. When she tried to engage the child in further conversation, the child just hummed and looked out the car window.

If you want to try this experiment, choose a time when the child is busy with another activity, playing, riding in the car, or perhaps as you are tucking him or her into bed at night. Be very casual in your approach.

Do children remember? We can only wonder, but as usual, fact is stranger than fiction.

It's So Easy!

While a friend and I were having dinner in a local Chinese restaurant, she began telling me of a strong flashback memory she had experienced. She knew that it was very important to a relationship she was involved in. So, between finishing dinner and getting the bill, I said to her, "Close your eyes, take a deep breath, go back there now, remember everything."

She looked at me quizzically and said, "Right now, here?"

"Yes, it's easy. Go ahead," I encouraged her.

She did as I suggested and began talking to me of this other life. She recalled amazing details and was able to see how the past life was affecting her current relationship. She's a very creative person, and I knew she could "remember" very easily. Because I encouraged her to trust herself, she had an eye-opening experience.

I'm always encouraging people to allow themselves to remember a past life, and sometimes even I'm surprised at what they come up with. While driving across high desert country one day with a friend of mine, he said, "There's a road just ahead that leads to a reservoir. Let's go see if we can find it."

I was driving and thought it would be fun to take a little side trip. The next little road off the main highway did not look promising, but because he wanted to see if this reservoir he had heard about was there, I pulled off the highway and proceeded down a very bumpy, graded road. The reservoir was there, and the setting was lovely. There were birch trees surrounding the reservoir. It was a quiet, peaceful place. We stood with arms around each other in the shade of the birch trees, enjoying the stillness and serenity of the moment. I said, "Take a deep breath and go back to another time when we've been together in a place like this."

Just minutes later he said, "That was the strangest experience. I saw us dressed in animal skins. We were racing up the side of a hill, trying to outrun the rising waters of a raging river below us."

"Did we make it?" I asked.

"No," he said, "we were killed by the rising waters. Oh well, at least we died together."

This was hardly what I expected to hear. I had hoped he would remember a picnic on the banks of a pretty lake, but it was his experience, not mine.

One woman who took a workshop based on the material in this book came to class one evening a little agitated. She said, "Elaine, I had the most startling experience after I was guided to a past life last week."

"By the look on your face, I can tell it's going to be interesting. What happened?" I asked.

"While I was washing my face and getting ready for bed, I looked into the mirror. The face reflected wasn't my face. It was the same face I saw as myself in the regression."

"I love it! What did you do?" I asked.

"I was so startled, I put my head back down over the sink and began splashing water on my face and taking deep breaths. When I next looked up, everything was normal. It was me in the mirror."

"You're a great subject," I told her. "Don't let yourself be afraid when something like that happens. Go with it and see what else you can remember. I've never had that happen—I envy you the experience."

"Oh, I think I'd do better with it now, it was just so surprising. I'll let you know if it happens again."

The most interesting story I've heard about the unexpected recall of a past life, was told one evening at a workshop. As the participants discussed strong feelings of déjà vu they had experienced, Marilyn related an incident that had occurred twelve years before. She had attended a three-week course at a small, private Catholic college. The campus held a lovely old mansion now occupied by nuns. One evening after dinner, while she and seven others from the class were strolling the campus, they came upon this house. As they stood outside and admired the once grand mansion, one of the nuns who resided there stepped out and asked if they would like a tour of the home. The group enthusiastically followed their hostess inside. As they entered they found themselves facing a magnificent double circular stairway. To their right were double doors that opened to the former ballroom. The nun invited them to explore the lower floor and excused herself. The group entered the ballroom. Inside was a piano. One of the men sat down and began to play the *Calvery Waltz*. As he played, the gentleman Marilyn was standing beside extended his hand and they began to waltz. As they did so, their perception of the room and each other began to shift and change. Both saw her clad in an elegant emerald green ball gown, and him in a grey uniform with yellow stripes down the sides of the pant legs, epaulets on his shoulders, and shiny brass buttons. As they continued to move with the moment, they both became aware of others who had been at the ball many years before. They could hear laughter and conversation, and could see the room filled with people.

As if this weren't amazing enough, the other five people in the group standing to the side all had the same vision. They too saw Marilyn's ball gown, his uniform, and all saw a lovely, ornate candelabra on the piano. It was as though a curtain in time parted and the entire group stepped through to relive a shared moment from another time. The vision ended abruptly for everyone when the nun who currently lived in the house stepped into the room and asked them not to play the piano. Needless to say, the remainder of that night was spent discussing and comparing notes about what had happened. No one came up with a plausible explanation, but each of them was aware they had experienced something highly unusual. Did they step through a veil in time? Was their friendship enough to transport them all back to a moment in time that they had shared more than a hundred years before? What happened?

All of these experiences were unexpected and unplanned. They were spontaneous opportunities for further insight. Allow yourself to be open to these kinds of experiences. Trust what comes to you. If it weren't important, you wouldn't remember. Pay attention.

Researching Past-Life Memories

If a past life you explore takes you to a recorded historical time, there are ways to investigate and validate some of the information you come up with. Visiting a state historical society can provide a unique window into the past. These societies are an excellent resource. You can find newspapers on microfilm, as well as old photographs of towns and people. There are often ledgers of business transactions and personal journals of people who lived in the area. Historical societies also collect artifacts such as hand-woven Indian baskets, tools, and other memorabilia. If you take the time to view some of these things, you might feel a familarity with them that goes beyond any knowledge you had prior to your regression.

The public library is another excellent resource for discovering period costumes around the globe. You can learn about the architecture of a specific time and place, the foods that were eaten, battles fought. In additional to historical records you can explore books on archeology and anthropology.

Perhaps visiting sites containing petroglyphs will evoke memories.

These are just a few ideas. You may be motivated to discover other ways to explore the past.

⊠   CHAPTER **8**

Using Self-Hypnosis for Past-Life Recall

Self-hypnosis is an amazing tool. It is the use of your mind in the most creative, productive way possible. With self-hypnosis you can gain access to subconscious information that will help you in the present.

I continue to be tickled when I'm introduced to someone new. If I'm introduced as, "This is my friend Elaine. She's a hypnotist," the reaction usually lets me know that what I do is still highly suspect in many people's eyes. The person I'm being introduced to usually laughs and says, "Oh, don't look into my eyes." or "Are you going to swing a watch in front of my face.?" Ah, to have that much power! The fact of the matter is, I don't. The power a hypnotist uses is the mind of the subject.

You have been entering and leaving self-induced hypnotic states (trances or altered states of consciousness) since the day you were born. You were in an altered state of consciousness last night when you lay down to go to sleep. As you relaxed your body, without any conscious effort or special knowledge from your conscious mind, you slowed down your cycle-per-second brain wave activity.

And then again as you awakened this morning, you moved from a slower brain wave pattern into a fully alert state. There is no more mystery or abracadraba in waking and sleeping than there is in self hypnosis. Changing brain patterns is a natural, inherent ability. Each of us possesses it. Everyone who chooses to can be hypnotized and can successfully work with self-hypnosis. Someone who doesn't want to be hypnotized is not a good subject.

The following are the brain wave activity levels and the states of consciousness they represent:

BETA	Fully conscious and alert
ALPHA	Hypnosis
	Meditation
	Awakening in the morning
	Falling to sleep at night
THETA	Deep hypnosis
	Deep meditation
	Crossing over into sleep at night
DELTA	Full sleep to deep sleep

That's it. There's no place else to go. You cannot get into a hypnotic state and get lost there. The worst that could happen is that, if you were working with self-hypnosis and were extremely tired, you might fall asleep, waking up when you were rested, or the phone rang, or when some other normal household sound awakened you.

People also are concerned that if they are hypnotized, they will be totally out of control. The fact is you are not under the control of anyone when you're hypnotized or using self-hypnosis. You are simply relaxed and in a heightened state of awareness, as opposed to being unconscious or unaware. I explain to my clients that if I were to hypnotize them and ask them to take my hand and walk out to the highway with me to see if the cars would hit us, they would simply open their eyes and tell me I could go alone. If they were really a deep-level subject, they would refuse to comply. When you're in hypnosis you cannot be made to do anything that violates your morals, religious beliefs, or instinct for self-preservation. Our mind has a built-in self-defense mechanism. We always have free choice.

Also, hypnosis does not act like a truth serum. Under hypnosis you will not reveal information that you would otherwise not divulge. If you are working with another person to explore a past life and details come to you that you would be uncomfortable sharing, you will edit your responses, just as you do in normal conversation.

Actually, the only time you are not being hypnotized *by others* is when you're in hypnosis. I feel safer in hypnosis than at any other time, because that is my time away from the world. I am not being "programmed" by the TV, the radio, friends, or clients. I am in a very relaxed, comfortable state of mind, open only to suggestions I choose to respond to. But I certainly cannot be made to remember anything against my will, or that would be harmful to me. Once again, the mind is an incredible device: it is designed to protect us, to allow only what we can deal with at the moment to come to our conscious awareness.

Have you ever had the experience of driving your car and arriving home only to think, "Good heavens, were the lights red or green? What route did I take?" If you've experienced that, and most people have, you experienced an altered state of consciousness, a light trance state that enabled you to drive and respond to the traffic, but to do so without absolute concentration on what you were doing. State driving manuals warn us to be aware of "road hypnosis," and that is what they are talking about.

Think of an injury you've experienced. You can remember the incident, but not the pain, or the sensation of the pain. Your mind has taken that memory from you to protect you. And so it works with regressive hypnosis. You will not recall anything that would be harmful to you. I have worked with many clients who were in great emotional pain as they ended a relationship. They had sought me out as a regressive hypnotist for help in understanding their situation. When I have directed them to the past life that would give them insight into the present, they block my suggestions and will not go back. Regardless of the techniques I use to push them back, they continue to resist, and I know they are not ready for that information. Often they return several months later and try again. Almost without fail, they go back to the past life they need to explore. Often the past life will be so like what they are experiencing in the present that it amazes them. They are then free of the limitations from the past and can deal more effectively with the present.

I Don't Think I Can Be Hypnotized

Often a client will say to me, "I have a very analytical mind. I don't think this will work for me." Or "I'm afraid to give up my control. Can I still do this?" "Yes," is always my reply. The more analytical your mind is, the more intelligent you are, the more creative you are, and the better subject you make. A little healthy skepticism never hurt anyone. I was very skeptical when I first used hypnosis. I would have bet money that it would not work for me. In spite of my doubt, it worked amazingly well. We all think we are the exception to the rule and believe that what works for others will never work for us. Or we feel that hypnosis is mysterious and otherworldly. But it's not. It is something you can experience right now, right where you are. No special tools are required. You were born with the equipment to be successful—your mind.

But I Saw a Stage Hypnotist . . .

If you have seen a hypnotist portrayed in a movie or on TV, what you saw probably bore little or no resemblance to reality. Stage hypnotism is another story. Stage hypnotists intend to entertain, not to educate, so everything they do is mysterious and leaves false impressions in the minds of the observers. First, the depth we attain in hypnosis is as individual as our thumb prints. Some people can go very deep, attaining a somnambulistic state. This simply refers to the cycle-per-second brain wave activity they are experiencing. About one person in ten is capable of achieving this depth. I am not one of those people, and yet I have successfully used hypnosis for years. So do not decide it won't work for you if you can't immediately achieve results. Working creatively with your mind is a learned, practiced skill. Just as you graduated from a three-wheel bike to a two-wheeler when you were a child, you can learn to use hypnosis effectively. Like any other skill or ability, the more you put into it, the more effective it will be.

I often hear of experiences with night club hypnotists who ask for volunteers from the audience. Once one of my clients was among about thirty others who eagerly approached the stage, wanting to take part in the show. The hypnotist sent all but three back to their seats. He had chosen to keep those who could attain a somnambulistic trance, first hypnotizing the entire group, carefully observing their responses to suggestion, and chosing the most suggestible. Those chosen then responded to his suggestions and barked like dogs or quacked like ducks. He suggested they could not get up from their chairs, and they were unable to do so. He also gave them the suggestion that later in the show when he said a key word, they would respond by jumping up and saying something outlandish. This got a big laugh from the audience and amazed the person who was the subject.

Keep in mind that none of the suggestions violated that person's morals, religious beliefs, or instinct for self-preservation. Had a suggestion been given that would have threatened the subject, he would have refused to comply, even though he was in an extremely deep trance. Tests have been conducted with somnambulistic-level subjects, and even they will not do *anything* they would not do fully awake and alert.

Actually, this should serve as an example of how powerful our minds are. Think how exciting it is to give yourself an opportunity to explore your mind while in hypnosis. Think what you can discover and accomplish with this tool. Realize also that you are on a new adventure, the exploration of your own mind.

How Does It Work?

When you enter hypnosis you are far more suggestible than you would be if you were in full beta consciousness. You can bypass your conscious, critical mind and retrieve memories directly from your subconscious. It is easier in this state to accept suggestions and to have memories of another life, because you are bypassing the conscious mind. That is not to say you are unaware; it is simply a method to gain access to the subconscious. Consider that we normally use five to ten percent of our mental capacity. The other ninety percent is waiting for us to give it direction, but we rarely do. Hypnosis provides an opportunity to take a suggestion forward with a quantum leap.

How Long Has This Been Going On?

One of the oldest archeological sites in France contains cave drawings clearly depicting people in altered states of consciousness. Human beings have always used altered states of consciousness. It is time for us to begin tapping into our own minds again. Einstein said he got his ideas "from mystical sources." I believe that is an indication that he spent time in an altered state of consciousness, because I don't believe it's possible to communicate with "mystical sources" any other way. Thomas Edison was noted for his cat naps. I don't think he was taking naps, I think he was altering his consciousness to receive solutions to the inventions he was currently working on, and to get more ideas. He must have been doing something right, because he obtained over 1,000 patents.

There are hundreds of examples of extraordinary people who have discovered ways to use their minds creatively. They may not have said they were practicing self-hypnosis, but the results they achieved indicate they were accessing their subconscious minds to heighten their creativity, to be inspired, and to execute wonderful concepts. For example, the singer John Denver was in Houston to do a benefit and memorial concert for the seven astronauts who died in the Challenger tragedy. I watched one of the television interviews and noted with interest his reply when he was asked how he had come to write his song "Flying Free," commemorating the astronauts. He said that when he watched the television accounts of the tragedy, he was touched and moved, and said, "As I often do when something happens that creates an emotional impact in my life, I picked up my guitar and played it as a meditation. The words and music were just there." Ah yes, I thought, as the words and music are there for so many creative people. Within each of us are the words and music that will enhance our own lives, give us solace, and a sense of awe at the world we live in. But first we must learn to be still, to tap into our minds, and to trust the images, words, and music that flow from them. We must be willing to journey to find the beauty within us. That is the challenge.

CHAPTER 9

Self-Hypnosis—Let's Begin

You are about to become one among a very special group of people who have learned how to tap into the magic of their own subconscious mind. You are embarking on an adventure that has no end, that will offer a multitude of opportunities for you to explore and to understand yourself. Inside of you is potential you have never realized existed, power you never knew you possessed. It's time to use it.

In order to gain the most from exploring past lives you need to release, just momentarily, your need to understand exactly what is happening. You can go into and beyond your mind, exploring limitless places. The trick is to give yourself permission to explore, to wonder, to think unlimited thoughts—to feel, once again, your own inner workings.

Those great thinkers who have preceded you, who believed they had lived before, have led the way for the rest of us. Walt Whitman, Henry Ford, Thomas Edison, and all those other brilliant minds, were thinkers first. Before they acted, they spent time thinking, considering, going beyond the limitations others imposed on themselves. And from their clear thinking, their ability to reach into the unknown, to risk, to dare, came wonderment for all of us. You must be willing to do the same thing. It will be a valuable exercise for you, a way to learn to trust yourself, to train your mind to go beyond the seeming limitations of physical space into new vistas, new awareness, new knowledge.

The first rule is, don't begin by deciding to try this inner exploration to see if it will work, or if it will help. The word *try* implies failure, and your subconscious mind is very literal. Instead program yourself as you begin with such thoughts as: "I will be successful. I will experiment, I will trust the impressions that come to me. I will learn more about myself."

While I was shopping in a local bookstore one afternoon, a woman approached me and asked, "Aren't you Elaine, the lady who does the past life regressions?"

"Yes, I am," I responded, smiling.

"I attended one of your group regressions about three months ago. I just wanted to tell you how much I enjoyed it and how I continue to be surprised at the things that pop into my head from that evening."

"Really? How nice. Tell me what you've been experiencing." I replied.

She then told me she is an artist and teaches art to children and adults. "When I did the regression," she said, "it showed me that I could trust the impressions that come to me. That trust has carried over into other areas of my life and allowed me to trust my direct perception of people and events. Drawing is a skill I've developed over many years. Before the regression, when I did a drawing easily and quickly, I would question its worth. I know now that was my left brain complaining because it wasn't needed in that process. Something else interesting: I still keep flashing back on that past life, or I see a movie or something on television that triggers a memory from it. I am amazed when it happens. I was an artist in that past life. That's why art is so important to me now."

"Great!" I replied. "Keep being aware of those flashes of insight from your mind. They're coming to you for a reason.

You are probably continuing to receive information because you're so open to it."

Before you begin to do regressive hypnosis, practice entering an altered state of consciousness daily for at least two weeks. It will give you confidence in your ability to use hypnosis. A good conditioning exercise to use in your practice sessions is to go mentally to a favorite place outdoors. Create every detail you can: the temperature, the time of day, the setting. Feel the sun touching your body, hear the sounds of the place, see every detail. If there are trees in the setting you choose, mentally hang a hammock and lie in it, observing everything around you. See what you are wearing. Add other people to this visualization, if you would like to have them there. Do this exercise consistently for two weeks to get the most benefit from it. The more you work with visualizing a favorite place, the easier it will be for you to experience memories from another time.

When I conduct a group past life regression, there is no opportunity for the participants to practice self-hypnosis before they attend the workshop. To help them have a successful regression, I lead a practice session. This gives them an opportunity to experience hypnosis, and to see how they will receive past life impressions. During the practice session I describe various outdoor scenes to them, and then very briefly suggest they will receive impressions of another life. Invariably there are those who "don't feel hypnotized." Others are amazed at what they've experienced. One man at the end of the practice session told me, "I was sure I couldn't be hypnotized and absolutely positive I would not receive any past life impressions. But when you told us to look down and be aware of what was on our feet, I saw armor. And then I could feel my whole body dressed in armor. You've got me now, there's something to this, I'm amazed."

I love it when someone who is so skeptical is successful in receiving impressions. The reason this man was successful was because he had an open mind, open enough to attend a workshop he felt sure he couldn't succeed with, but at least he was game enough to try. It was his willingness to try that allowed him to have his experience. You can do the same thing. Give yourself permission to try.

The following steps will guide you into an altered state. Try it. You'll see how easy it is.

Inducing Self-Hypnosis

1. *Find a quiet place* where you will not be disturbed for fifteen or twenty minutes. I suggest you unplug the phone. Just knowing it won't ring is relaxing.
2. *Make yourself comfortable.* Kick off your shoes. Loosen any tight clothing. If you wear contact lenses and usually remove them for a nap, take them out for self hypnosis. You will be more comfortable without them.
3. *Take long, slow, deep breaths.* Imagine you are inhaling peaceful, tranquil feelings and instruct yourself to exhale all tension from your body and mind. If you hold tension in your jaw, neck, and shoulders, consciously loosen this entire area as you breathe out, letting your head bob forward for a moment, leave a space between your teeth. Breathe deep . . . exhale . . . relax. Continue breathing deeply, relaxing more and more with each breath. As you breathe deeply, gently allow your eyes to close. This eliminates visual stimulation and enhances your ability to tune into yourself.
4. *Imagine a relaxing power moving through your body.* Feel this relaxing power, sense it, direct it, become aware of your body. Be systematic, concentrate on this relaxing power, imagine it as a light flowing through your body. Until you sat down to practice self-hypnosis, you probably

spent the day racing around, totally unaware of your physical body. Now is the time to notice your body, to become aware of every muscle, every fiber, every cell, and every atom. It's time to tune in to yourself, to allow the rest of the world to float and drift away.

Continue to imagine this relaxing power moving through your body. Don't just think about it. Feel it, direct it, allow it, flow into it. See and feel this relaxing power moving up your legs, *feel* them relax. Feel your hips relax, now moving this relaxing power into both of your hands, *feel* your hands relax, and then your arms. Now slowly move this relaxing power up your spine, and then direct your shoulders to become loose and limp, very loose and limp, then feel the relaxing power moving up your neck and scalp, then flowing across your face, relaxing the muscles around your eyes and your mouth, relaxing your jaw to allow a space between your teeth.

5. *Scan your body from the top of your head to your toes* for a few moments. If you detect any area that is not completely relaxed, simply direct that area to become totally relaxed.

6. *Visualize your body being surrounded with a circle of protective white light.* This is a mental protective device. It is a "White God light." By surrounding yourself with this light you have totally sealed yourself off from any negative energy in your environment. You can relax and know that you are protected while you are experiencing self hypnosis.

7. *Begin slowly and rhythmically to count backward from seven to one, to deepen your state of relaxation.* As you do so, direct yourself to go deeper and deeper into relaxation. Say to yourself, "Seven, deeper, deeper, deeper, down, down, down, six deeper, deeper, deeper, down, down, down," and so on, till you reach one. Then pause a mo-

ment, sense how relaxed you feel, and then direct yourself to relax even further, again counting backward from seven to one, suggesting you are going deeper and deeper.

An easy way to send yourself deeper into relaxation is to imagine you are walking down a flight of stairs, or riding down in an elevator, watching the numbers of the floors as you descend. My clients have come up with some interesting deepening techniques to enhance the backward count. You might try some of them, or create your own. One woman, an avid skier, saw herself skiing downhill, and imagined she was going very quickly and smoothly. Another client, a deep sea diver, saw himself in a diving bell floating down into very deep water. Another man saw himself descending carved stone steps; he even saw the steps turn a corner, which he "knew" he could turn and continue descending.

Once again: it's your trip, so be creative and imagine what works best for you. I find it very helpful to just imagine I am going very deep inside myself, feeling the physical world dissolve as I tune into my inner being.

By the time you go through the second count down, you will be very relaxed, and you will have altered your brain wave pattern. *The earth will not move.* Nothing extraordinary will happen to indicate to you that you are in hypnosis. So often when I work with people, even though they are excellent subjects, even though they were definitely experiencing an altered state of consciousness, they still doubted it. This does not mean that just a few people have this doubt. At least 50 percent of the people I work with never feel hypnotized. Everyone has preconceived ideas of what being hypnotized feels like, and since what they are experiencing bears no resemblance to what they've seen on TV or at the movies, they're sure they have not achieved a state of hypnosis. Now this is the important part. *Trust yourself.* I'll say it again: *trust yourself, trust the process, know that you are being successful.*

Below are some physiological indications of an altered state of consciousness. You may experience one or more of them. Remember, you are unique, and your experience is your own.

1. A feeling of deep relaxation.
2. A slight tingling in your arms or legs.
3. A feeling of heaviness in your arms or legs, or perhaps your entire body. You may have felt that you were going to sink right through your chair or couch.
4. Rapid movement of your eyes behind closed eyelids. This is called REM activity, and is the same thing noted in laboratories when dream states are studied.
5. Inability to determine if the process took five minutes or twenty minutes. Very often when we are in an altered state of consciousness we are removed from our conscious, critical mind and not aware of time the same way as when we are not in hypnosis.

In an altered state you can suggest to yourself that you have twenty minutes to devote to self hypnosis and that in precisely twenty minutes you will bring yourself up and out of trance. Even though we consciously are not aware of a time frame, our subconscious readily accepts such instructions. If you feel uncertain of yourself, set a timer for twenty minutes. Then relax and allow yourself to enjoy the trip.

You will probably notice while you're in hypnosis that your mind does not turn off. Even though you are imagining a place in nature, that left-brain, linear part of your mind will be thinking, "I should have stopped at the store. We're out of milk and bread" or some other totally unrelated thought. Do not be concerned. This does not mean you're not in hypnosis. Allow those thoughts to fade into the background and be aware of the images in your mind. If you consciously resist those thoughts you will pull yourself out of self-hypnosis. Just relax and allow the process to work for you.

Be aware also that you may find it difficult to create a perfectly quiet time to practice self-hypnosis, but absolute quiet is not necessary. I was working with a client in a private session one morning in my office. Construction workers on the floor above us chose that moment to begin hammering. I continued the session, thinking to myself it was a fruitless endeavor. Since she did not open her eyes and ask what was going on, I continued. After the session I told her, "I apologize for the racket. I have no control over what they're doing up there. I'll be happy to schedule another appointment for you and do your hypnosis session under quieter circumstances."

"Oh, don't worry," she said, "I was faintly aware of the noise, but it just wasn't important. I barely heard it."

I'm not suggesting that you practice self hypnosis in the middle of a construction site, or in a nursery school playground, just that you do not have to have an absolutely quiet, darkened room. I tell my clients, "I can't turn the world off for you while you're here, and you can't turn it off when you leave, so use any noise you hear to relax you further. Do not allow yourself to be disturbed."

Eye Fixation Technique

Another method to enter an altered state of consciousness is called an eye fixation technique. It is easily accomplished, and one that you probably associate with hypnosis. When stage hypnotists ask subjects to stare at a fixed point in front of them, they are using this technique. To practice this technique, sit quietly for a few moments, then begin to breathe deeply and completely. You can stare at any object you choose. Your thumbnail is readily available, so it is an easy way to begin. Sit with your hands in your lap, your thumbnail facing you. Fix your gaze on your thumbnail, suggesting to yourself as you do, "My eyes are getting heavy, I'm feeling more relaxed each moment." Continue repeating this phrase until your eyes become very tired, and then allow them to close. As you close your eyes, begin telling yourself, "I am drifting into a very deep state of relaxation, going deeper and deeper with each breath." Then allow and direct yourself to drift deeper and deeper, feeling more and more relaxed as you do so. In just a few short minutes you will have achieved an altered state of consciousness.

As you practice with self-hypnosis techniques, you will become conditioned to easily achieve an altered state of consciousness. To further enhance your ability to quickly move into an altered state, give yourself the following suggestion each time you practice: "I will go deeper and faster each time I practice self-hypnosis."

You may find your ability to enter a trance state more helpful than you realize. One evening when I was working with a small group of people in my home, one of the gentlemen present began searching the floor around his seat. He continued to look around unobtrusively, so I stopped what I was doing and asked him what the problem was. He explained that he had just lost his contact lens. It must have popped out of his eye. Everyone then began to search for his contact lens. We found every piece of lint and cat hair on the carpeting, but no lens. He was beginning to be uncomfortable about the amount of time and attention his problem was taking from the class and our purpose and asked us to continue with the class—he would get another contact lens.

"Wait, just a moment," I suggested. "Since you've learned self hypnosis, let's take a few moments and see if you can discover where that lens is, even though you consciously do not have any idea where it is. I have another suggestion. Your subconscious knows where it is. Let's find it."

"Oh, all right," he replied. He didn't seem convinced hypnosis would help, but was willing to give it a try. I quickly guided him into an altered state and directed him to remember when he was last aware of seeing through the contact lens. I then instructed him that on the count of three, he would know exactly where it was now and, as soon as he opened his eyes, would retrieve the lens. When I brought him out of hypnosis he said, "I think it's still in my eye. But I've looked for it and couldn't see it in there." His wife, who was also attending the workshop, carefully pulled his eyelid up, and sure enough, there was the contact lens.

After the class one of the other students said to me. "You really put yourself on the line tonight. Wouldn't you have felt a little foolish if he hadn't found that contact lens?"

"No," I replied. "I know how the mind works, and I knew he would be able to find it if we tried hypnosis. I really do trust what comes from the mind. It can be depended upon, almost without fail."

I'm Hypnotized—Now What?

Now it is time to give yourself some very positive suggestions about your ability to remember your past lives. It is important that the suggestions you give yourself be well thought out and worded in a positive way. An excellent suggestion would be: "I am practicing visualizing my favorite place in nature. I am doing this to prepare myself for a very successful experience with regressive hypnosis."

Many times I work with people who are not visual. When I ask them, "What do you see when you close your eyes?" Their answer is, "Nothing, it's just black." If that is the case with you, it's all right. You may be more auditory than visual in how you receive information. So say the words in your mind, talk to yourself about the memories you recall, the past lives you remember. You will probably find that within a few weeks of working with self-hypnosis you begin to be more visual, as you activate that part of your mind. Do not be concerned if you do not "see" the pictures you are creating. The words are as powerful as the images. Again, do what works for you.

Even though you may not feel hypnotized, simply allow yourself to relax and enjoy the time you have created for yourself. You will always achieve at least a light altered state, and you will benefit from being in this state. You are giving yourself an opportunity to get in touch with your right brain, that creative part of yourself.

A friend of mine, a businessman who tends to push himself too hard, has discovered an extremely good technique that is a form of self-hypnosis. He has programmed himself to receive solutions to business problems while he's in the shower. As he's going off to sleep at night, he suggests to himself, "In the morning, I will get new ideas and solutions." He then specifically states which items he needs an answer to. This is a great technique, because it enables him to sleep well. And because he has used this technique successfully for years, he tends to be very creative in his problem-solving abilities. I was so impressed when he told me about this technique that I began using it myself. Many of the ideas for this book came from those flashes of insight I received in the shower. When I asked my friend if he realized that what he had been doing constituted self-hypnosis, he was surprised. He had never thought of it that way. In fact, many people may use this simple process; it's one that we've all found ways to use, we've just never identified what we're doing as using self-hypnosis.

Bringing Yourself out of Hypnosis

You will always come back from hypnosis, just as you have always snapped back from a daydream. If you should find yourself lingering for a little while longer in trance, it is only because you choose to do so since you find it so pleasant. You may want to enjoy this sense of deep peace and relaxation for a few more minutes before awakening. However, when you're ready, simply desiring to "come up" is sufficient. When you wish to return to full beta consciousness, you will. Be aware that any normal household sound, and most certainly anything that requires your immediate attention, will bring you out of hypnosis. You will be able to respond as quickly to the word *fire* as anyone else. I always tell my clients, "Don't worry—if the building's on fire, you'll beat me to the door."

Use a one to five count to bring yourself up. Tell yourself, "On the count of five I'll open my eyes and be wide awake, feeling refreshed, relaxed, and revitalized." Use these suggestions: "Number one—coming up a little, feel very good all over; number two—coming up a little more, feeling relaxed and refreshed; number three—feeling completely revitalized; number four—head clear, mind sharp; number five—eyes open, feeling wide awake and very good all over." Then take a few moments to reorient yourself to your surroundings.

As you can see, you do not have to go to the high Himalayas and study with monks to learn self-hypnosis. It is a simple tool, readily available, and not at all mysterious.

Can Something Go Wrong?

Nothing can go wrong while you're in hypnosis. You are working with your own mind. It is designed to protect and help you. Nothing will happen that will create a problem for you. As a matter of fact, you really are in control of what is happening. I witnessed a convincing demonstration of that control several years ago. I was attending an advanced three-day intensive training seminar for hypnotists. The teacher was instructing us in what he called "ultra-depth" or "coma" levels of hypnosis. His subject was his colleague, a woman who had been part of his business for the past thirty years, who demonstrated her ability to achieve this level of trance.

Several physicians were in attendance. They checked her motor responses and the dilation of her eyes. She was totally unaware of their presence and not bothered at all by their testing and observing. Throughout all the testing she maintained exactly the position she had been placed in. She was sitting on a straight-back chair, with her arms extended at shoulder height in front of her and her legs extended straight out at the height of the chair seat—a position I could not maintain for more than a few moments, but which seemed to require no effort on her part.

The teacher had instructed her to enter this state when he spoke the word *elephant*. When he brought her out of this deep state of hypnosis, we all of course asked if his saying the trigger word *elephant* could cause her to inadvertently go into this deep state. He told us that was not possible and demonstrated this by saying the word *elephant* several times. She would not respond to the word unless she chose to.

He stressed that she was always in complete control. To further make his point he told us about an incident that took place while they were attending a hypnosis convention. One evening he and several other hypnotists had gathered in his hotel room for a demonstration of this coma state. His colleague entered the deep trance state on command. Moments later, she spontaneously snapped out of hypnosis saying, "I smell smoke." They were on the twenty-second story of a hotel. No one else in the room was able to detect smoke in the air. She insisted there was smoke in the hotel, so they called the manager, who surprised everyone when he said, "There was a small fire in a waste basket on the seventh floor. It has been extinguished, and there is no danger."

Clearly, our perceptions and senses are heightened in hypnosis. The deeper we allow ourselves to drift into hypnosis, the more keenly we are aware of our surroundings and the sharper our perceptions.

There are no problems inherent in hypnosis, there is only opportunity to be more aware, more in control, more knowledgeable of your inner workings. To insure your success, do not work at it. Simply allow yourself to drift and float, to relax very deeply. The less you try, the easier it is.

Creating a Relaxation Tape

When I teach self hypnosis I always provide an audio tape for the participants to listen to. It is much easier to listen to a tape than to sit down and go through the process into relaxation on your own. After working with a tape for just a couple of weeks, people are conditioned to the relaxation response and quickly and easily achieve an altered state. The following is a script for you to read onto a cassette tape. I have written the script to help you become proficient at visualizing and feeling a place and to help you practice being in another place in time. Practice reading the script through before you record it. It should be read in a slow, rhythmic manner in a calm voice. You will find it relaxing to create the tape, and even more relaxing as you work with it.

One note of caution: do not play the tape while driving or riding in a car. You need to be very alert to drive, and this tape is designed to create a deep sense of relaxation. Don't play it while you're driving.

Relaxation and Imagery Script

Begin by taking some slow, deep breaths and allowing your eyes to close. Imagine yourself inhaling peaceful, calm feelings and exhaling all tension from your body and mind. Breathe deeply and fully now, allowing yourself to relax completely, becoming calm, slowing down your mind, relaxing your body. This is your time to restore yourself at all levels, physically, mentally, emotionally, and spiritually. Maximize this time, allowing yourself to relax completely, as you continue to breathe deeply and calmly. As you breathe deeply, begin imagining your entire body relaxing, sensing a relaxing power moving into the toes of both of your feet. Feel this relaxing power moving through your feet and up into your legs, totally relaxing your legs, totally relaxing your lower legs and your upper legs. You are beginning to feel very relaxed, to feel safe and comfortable now, as this relaxing power continues to move up into your hips. Now your hips are relaxed. Now feel this relaxing power flowing into the fingers of both of your hands, relaxing your hands. Feel it flowing up into your arms, relaxing your arms totally. Now imagine this relaxing power slowly and gently moving up your spine, feel it as a warm current, relaxing your entire body and spreading out across your shoulders, allowing them to be very loose and limp. Feel this relaxing power now moving up your neck, relaxing your neck, and then moving across your scalp and down into your face, allowing the muscles to relax around your eyes and your mouth. Allow your jaw to relax and feel a little space between your teeth. Your entire body is now relaxed, your mind is calm, you are feeling very good all over. Now take a moment and, starting at the top of your head, begin to scan your body. If any part of your body is not relaxed, simply direct it to become completely relaxed. Do this now.

[*Pause a few moments.*]

And now with the power of your mind, feel a circle of white protective light totally surrounding your body and mind. Sense it, see it, and feel it. It is there.

[*Pause again a few moments.*]

You are now totally protected. Continue breathing deeply and completely, imagining you are inhaling light, knowledge, and peacefulness.

And now as I count backward from seven to one, you will feel yourself drifting into a very deep, natural altered state. Allow and direct yourself to drift into a very deep, relaxing state: number seven—deeper, deeper, deeper, down, down, down; number six—deeper, deeper, deeper, down, down, down; number five—deeper, deeper, deeper, down, down, down; number four—deeper, deeper, deeper, down, down, down; number three—deeper, deeper, deeper, down, down, down; number two—deeper, deeper, deeper, down, down, down; number one. You are now in a very deep, peaceful level of consciousness, and you will continue to go even deeper with each breath.

Each time you consciously decide to be hypnotized, or to use self hypnosis techniques, you will always go deeper and faster than the time before. This is a deep state of relaxation you can easily re-experience any time you choose for any positive purpose. If you find yourself uncomfortable for any reason, you have the ability to bring yourself out of hypnosis simply by choosing to do so. You can count quickly up from one to five, easily returning to full beta consciousness.

You are relaxed now, feeling calm, safe, and comfortable. Each breath continues to guide you even deeper into relaxation. As you relax more and more now, begin to drift to a very peaceful place in nature. Begin to imagine yourself in the place outdoors where you have felt the most peaceful. Create that place in your mind very vividly: feel the ground beneath your feet, see the sky overhead, feel the air as it touches your face. Imagine every detail of this place, be there now.

[*Allow a quiet space of about two minutes.*]

You are drifting even deeper now; all tension is dissolved, your mind is free, your body relaxed. And now you give yourself permission to create an imaginary time from long, long ago. You can create an imaginery time in which you lived. It will be a very happy time, a time of self-knowledge and great peace. You can easily allow yourself to do this now. On the count of three you will be in another time and place, you will sense and see and feel yourself there. One, two, three. You are now there: be aware of your surroundings, how you are dressed, how do you feel? Be there now.

[*Allow a quiet space of about two minutes.*]

You have just successfully used your imagination to take yourself to another time and place. This is easy for you to do. You become better at doing this exercise each time you work with your tape. You trust yourself completely. You are learning to explore your own mind, to expand your horizons. Each time you work with your tape the impressions you receive will be more and more vivid.

You will bring all of these peaceful, calm feelings with you now into your life. On the count of five you'll open your eyes and be wide awake, feeling very refreshed, relaxed, and full of energy. Your mind will be sharp and clear. Number one—coming up, feeling very, very good; number two—coming up a little more, feeling relaxed and refreshed; number three—feeling completely revitalized; number four—head clear, mind sharp; number five—eyes open, feeling wide awake and very good all over.

Take a few moments to reorient yourself to your surroundings. To make yourself more comfortable, you can use a blanket to cover yourself while you are in hypnosis. Because you are very relaxed while in hypnosis, you may find yourself feeling a little chilled. Also, being covered gives you a sense of protection, thus enhancing your ability to relax.

Approach this time of relaxation very playfully. Do not make it work. Allow it to be fun.

CHAPTER 10

How Will I Receive Past-Life Impressions?

Just as each of us has a unique thumbprint, so each person receives past life impressions a little differently. There is no right or wrong way to receive information. For some it's a very vivid experience, like watching a movie. Such people will see things through the eyes of the person they once were. They will feel that whoever is guiding them through the experience is just a little slow for not knowing what is happening. They will speak in the first person, reliving past life events. What's happening is perfectly obvious to them, and should be, they feel, to anyone else.

One man who had this experience told me, "It was all in living color, only I wasn't watching, I was there. It felt as if someone else was behind my eyes, as if someone else was using my eyes. Then when I saw the sumptuous dining scene, I was there at the table, viewing the other people and room through my eyes."

One woman described her experience this way: "It was like looking at a TV screen that got more vivid as the experience unfolded. At the beginning it was as if I was watching through a telescope, and then as we continued the image began to get closer. I thought, this is ridiculous, I'm not really seeing this. But then I decided, oh well, I'll just go with this.

Once I made that decision, I began to have strong feelings about what I was viewing."

Other people receive only vague impressions. They may have a dim awareness of the size of the room they are in and the clothing they are wearing, but for the most part they will simply "feel" what is happening. Their replies to specific questions about their surroundings are vague. Since an in-depth past life exploration takes about an hour, it's obvious that only specific important events come to the surface. More important than *what* you remember is *how you feel* about the event, how you responded at that time. Minute details are not important. For instance, one woman who received incredible insight from her regression said, "Sometimes I see a quick picture. Sometimes the answer is just there. Other times, I know the answer in words. No matter how it comes to me, I always feel as if I'm making it up."

Other subjects will not see or feel anything in regressive hypnosis. They will simply know what is happening, just as they know their name in their current life. A certain amount of trust is required for anyone to experience a regression. Even more is required for the subject who receives no visual impressions.

One woman who found herself in colonial America said, "I was very aware of feeling unwashed. My hair was dirty; I felt sticky and sweaty. I felt uncomfortable, but I knew he [she had been a man in the previous life] was comfortable in that state. Also, the mannerisms were so real. I could feel myself fidgeting with my glasses. In the last scene, when I was in my home, I could feel my contentment with my wife and home life in general. I saw the rocks of the fireplace; it was as if I was actually sitting before that huge fireplace. Overall, it wasn't true because of anything I saw; it was just *true*. It was like hearing someone say the sky is blue—you know that to be true. My perception was from the back of my head. Rather than seeing with my eyes, I perceived from the back of my head. I felt as if I was making it all up, but if I sat down to write a story I couldn't come up with those kinds of details or continuity."

For a friend of mine who had a terrible time allowing herself to receive past life impressions, it was a real revelation the day she actually allowed it to happen. She said, "Sometimes it was vivid. Other times words would come to my head. I remember the hot sun. It was so hot. When you moved me to the last day of my life I could feel I was very old. I just knew that he [the man she had been] was in special ceremonial clothes for death. It was a very comfortable feeling."

Another client said she received impressions, "visually, with no sound. It was an intuitive awareness of the communication within the scene. When you asked questions of me, the answers were discernable from what was unfolding."

She said, "I had total comprehension of the scene, what had happened before, at the moment and after, in response to your questions."

The key element to success in a regression is to trust the experience. Regardless of how each of us receives past life impressions, they are impressions from our own mind and therefore deserve to be honored. To scoff at what comes from within you is totally counterproductive.

It's interesting for me to talk with people several months after they have taken my past lives workshop and to discover how the process is unfolding for them. One woman said, "My first experience was confusing. I expected to be more unaware of my surroundings while I was in hypnosis. I was trying too hard and not trusting my first impressions. When I realized those impressions were the past life, it was easy. The hardest part for me was trusting what I received. It was when I let myself really relax that I began experiencing the feelings from the other life, which has been the most valuable part of the experience for me."

For myself, I have learned over the years that the images in my mind have great value for me. Even though I am a very visual person, when I experience a past life regression, I feel the situations. I can feel the clothing I'm wearing. I can actually feel if I'm wearing a homespun cotton shirt or fine silk. In one of my past lives I was an American Indian woman. I could feel the soft buckskin of a special ceremonial dress I wore. I knew that it had elaborate beading on it, that it was white, that it had fringe. I could feel the fringe touching my arms and legs as I moved, could sense the ground beneath my feet. Even though I did not see the dress as I would if I were looking at a photograph, I knew exactly how it looked, and more important, how it felt on me. In that particular regression I had a child who was seriously ill. I felt myself kneeling over the child, holding up my hands to call the wind. As I called the wind, I knew it contained the healing power I needed for my child. Interestingly enough, when I asked an Apache medicine woman about this experience, she told me her people use the wind for healing. With experiences like that, it is hard to doubt the validity of what you receive.

A young woman I did a past life regression with went to a lifetime in England. During the regression she gave many details about her life. She said she worked for a newspaper called the *Telegraph*. She described her clothing and her hairstyle. She knew the year. After the session she felt that some of the historical facts she received were incorrect. She went to the public library to research her experience. She discovered that the newspaper *was* called the *Telegraph*. While at the library she also checked on costumes for that specific period. She believed that the dresses she saw were cut too narrow and that the hairstyle she observed couldn't be right. Much to her surprise, the dress she saw and the hairstyle were historically accurate.

When I first began working with regressive hypnosis, I spent as much time at the library as I did conducting regressions. Time and again historical facts checked out. I verified enough facts to satisfy myself that something most unusual was occurring and that my subjects were not fabricating the stories I heard. I then began to realize that what each person felt during their experience was far more important than their historical accuracy. The value in experiencing a regression lies in the understanding gained about the present.

The more you work with regressive hypnosis, the more you learn to trust yourself and the more information you receive. We have been raised in a technologically oriented society. We trust what can be put into a computer or on a slide rule, but we have not been trained to trust our own minds. When you start working with your mind, and with regressive hypnosis, this technology is of no use whatsoever. You have to allow yourself to put aside your conscious, critical mind and trust completely the images, impressions, and feelings that float up from your subconscious. What you experience is uniquely your own. In all the classes I've conducted, in all the private sessions I've done, I've never heard the same story twice.

Your regression will have as much meaning for you as you allow. It's your journey—take it with your heart and mind open so you will benefit in your present life. The greatest benefit will come from allowing yourself to use in the present the knowledge and wisdom gained from another time and place. Reflect on what you receive, be open to your own inner guidance. What are these images and impressions telling you? Is there a lesson you need to learn, something your own subconscious wants you to be aware of? If you approach exploring the past as an adventure, you'll probably discover a childhood interest—a movie you've seen again and again or a book you've read over and over. Those stories spoke to that part of you that wants to remember, that wants to learn and grow. As you experience a regression you may feel as if you are making it all up. Allow yourself to put that thought aside and trust what comes to you. The time to process the material you receive is after you've had the experience. Allow the information to help you.

CHAPTER **11**

How to Create an Audiotape for Past-Life Recall

There are several ways to begin the process of recalling past lives. By completing the exercises in the previous
chapters, you have been preparing yourself to be successful
with past-life exploration. Below is a list of basic guidelines:

1. Choose a time when you will not be interrupted.
2. Be as open as you possibly can, telling yourself that
   you will set aside your conscious, critical mind for the
   present.
3. Decide what aspect of your life you wish to explore. Be
   very clear about the purpose of the exploration. The
   more clearly you define your purpose, the more clearly
   you will receive guidance and information from your
   own mind.

You are creating an island in time and space for yourself,
a safe place for the most fascinating journey you will ever
take. You can begin by creating a cassette audiotape guiding
you to the lifetime you want to explore. The following is a
script for you to read onto a tape. It should be read in a slow,
rhythmic manner, in a calm voice. You may be more comfortable practicing a few times before you record the tape.

Past-Life Regression Script

Begin by taking some slow, deep breaths and allowing your eyes to close. Imagine yourself inhaling peaceful, calm feelings and exhaling all tension from your body and mind. Breathe deeply and fully now, allowing yourself to relax completely, becoming calm, slowing down your mind, relaxing your body. This is your time to restore yourself at all levels, physically, mentally, emotionally, and spiritually. Maximize this time, allowing yourself to relax completely, as you continue to breathe deeply and calmly. As you breathe deeply, begin imagining your entire body relaxing, sensing a relaxing power moving into the toes of both of your feet. Feel this relaxing power moving through your feet and up into your legs, totally relaxing your lower legs and your upper legs. You are beginning to feel very relaxed, to feel safe and comfortable now, as this relaxing power continues to move up into your hips. Now your hips are relaxed. Now feel this relaxing power flowing into the fingers of both of your hands, relaxing your hands. Feel it flowing up into your arms, relaxing your arms totally. Now imagine this relaxing power slowly and gently moving up your spine, feel it as a warm current, relaxing your entire body and spreading out across your shoulders, allowing them to be very loose and limp. Feel this relaxing power now moving up your neck, relaxing your neck, and then flowing across your scalp and down into your face, allowing the muscles to relax around your eyes and your mouth. Allow your jaw to relax and feel a little space between your teeth. Your entire body is now relaxed, your mind is calm, you are feeling very good all over. Now take a moment and, starting at the top of your head, begin to scan your body. If any part of your body is not relaxed, simply direct it to become completely relaxed. Do this now.

[*Pause a few moments.*]

And now with the power of your mind, sense a circle of white protective light totally surrounding your body and mind. Sense it, see it, and feel it.

[*Pause again a few moments.*]

You are now totally protected. Continue breathing deeply and calmly, imagining you are inhaling light, knowledge, and peacefulness.

And now as I count backward from seven to one, you will feel yourself drifting into a very deep, natural altered state. Allow and direct yourself to drift into a very deep, relaxing state: number seven—deeper, deeper, deeper, down, down, down; number six—deeper, deeper, deeper, down, down, down; number five—deeper, deeper, deeper, down, down, down; number four—deeper, deeper, deeper, down, down, down; number three—deeper, deeper, deeper, down, down, down; number two—deeper, deeper, deeper, down, down, down; number one. You are now in a very deep, peaceful level of consciousness, and you will continue to go even deeper with each breath.

[*If you choose, you can repeat the backward count, guiding yourself even deeper. If you have been practicing the techniques for relaxation in chapter 9, this will probably not be necessary.*]

Each time you consciously decide to be hypnotized, or to use self-hypnosis techniques, you will always go deeper and faster than the time before. This is a deep state of relaxation you can easily re-experience any time you choose for any positive purpose. If you find yourself uncomfortable for any reason, you have the ability to bring yourself out of hypnosis simply by choosing to do so. You can count quickly up from one to five, quickly and easily returning to full beta consciousness.

Within your mind are memories of everything that has ever happened to you, both in this life and in all of your previous incarnations. You can easily and effortlessly allow these memories to come back to your conscious mind. We are going to move back in time now, to another time and another place. I will count backward from five to one, and as I count you will allow yourself to move in time to a previous lifetime, trusting yourself completely. You are seeking information that will give you insight and understanding into your present life and circumstances.

Allow your mind to choose the lifetime to explore that will give you the most insight into your relationship with [use the name of the person or specifically state the issue you want to explore], trusting yourself completely now. Number five—beginning to move back in time, to another time and place; number four—moving on back, allowing it to happen, trusting completely; number three—your own mind choosing the lifetime you most need to explore at this time, the lifetime that will give you insight and understanding into the present and your relationship with [use name of person or specifically state the issue you want to explore]; number two—on the next count you will be there. You will be in another time and place, vivid impressions will come to your mind. Number one—you are now there, vivid impressions are coming in. Where are you, outside or inside?

[*Allow a quiet space of about one minute.*]

Sense and feel the place you are in, allow yourself to be very aware of your surroundings.

[*Allow a quiet space of about one minute.*]

And now become aware of how you are dressed, look down at your feet and feel what is on your feet and how you are dressed.

[*Allow a quiet space of about one minute.*]

Are you male or female?

[*Allow a quiet space of thirty seconds.*]

Be aware now of this particular day. On the count of three you will be aware of the significance of the particular day you have gone to. One, two, three. What is happening?

[*Allow a quiet space of about two minutes.*]

Go forward to a time when you are with another person, someone important to you. One, two, three. You are now there. What is happening?

[*Allow a quiet space of about two minutes.*]

How do you feel about this person? What is your relationship?

[*Allow a quiet space of about one minute.*]

What country or geographical location are you in?

[*Allow a quiet space of thirty seconds.*]

Move to a significant event that will provide you with more insight. On the count of three, move forward in time to a significant event. One, two, three. You are now there and vivid impressions are coming into your mind. Exactly what is happening?

[*Allow a quiet space of two minutes.*]

What is your name? Hear your name spoken. What are you called?

[*Allow a quiet space of thirty seconds.*]

Move now to another important event in the life you are reviewing. On the count of three move forward in time to a specific, important event. One, two, three. Where are you and exactly what is happening?

[*Allow a quiet space of two minutes.*]

You will have total, vivid recall of everything you have experienced. You release now at conscious and subconscious levels all limitations from the past life you have explored. You bring forward with you into your present life all the wisdom, knowledge, and understanding gained. On the count of five now you will move up into the highest levels of your own mind. Number one—moving up, feel it happening; number two—you are moving into the highest levels of your mind; number three—leaving the physical world behind; number four—on the next count you will be in the highest levels of your mind, with an expanded awareness of the past life you have just reviewed; number five—you are now there. From this expanded perspective, what was the purpose or lesson learned in the life you have just reviewed?

[*Leave one minute of quiet time.*]

And now look into the eyes of any person from that other time, look into his or her eyes and be aware if this is someone you know in the present.

[*Leave about one minute.*]

You will have total, vivid recall of all you've experienced. In the next few days, in moments of quiet reflection, in reverie or perhaps even in a dream, if there is additional information that will be helpful to you, it will come into your conscious mind. You will recognize this information and use it in your life. You have opened your mind to your own inner awareness. You will use this information to help yourself. You will have total, vivid recall of all you've experienced.

On the count of five you will open your eyes and be wide awake, feeling refreshed, relaxed, and revitalized. Number one—coming up, feeling very good; number two—having total recall of all you've experienced; number three—relaxed and calm, feeling very good all over; number four—on the next count you'll open your eyes and feel very good; number five—eyes open, feeling very good.

You can create as many tapes as you like. They can be used to explore relationships, career information, an interest or hobby, whatever you wish. It is best to put only one subject on a tape. Do not try to explore in one session your relationship with your husband/wife, your career, and your fear of heights. Chapter 12 contains a list of suggested past lives to explore, including questions to ask. Also, be aware that more than one past life may be affecting any specific area you want to explore. Sometimes several past lives affect one relationship, so do not assume that one regression will give you all the insight necessary to understand a particular situation.

If you have difficulty seeing the correlation between the past life you explored and your present life, talk with a friend about your experience. Someone who knows us well may often be more objective about our experience than we are and may more readily see the correlation between the past and present. Be as honest with yourself as you can about your experience. Realize that the past can teach you, can set you free.

Before you begin your session, have pen and paper ready to record your impressions. You will find that after your regression many other memories will float up to your conscious mind. Do pay attention to them. They have value.

As with any hypnosis tape, do not play it in a moving automobile.

CHAPTER 12

How to Work With a Friend

If you decide to explore your past lives with a friend, make certain you choose someone you trust completely. They must understand the process, your purpose, and be willing to be open to what is happening.

The first time I guided another person to a past life I was reading from a prepared script. It was one of the most amazing experiences of my life. The person I worked with was my brother Larry. He has always been a willing subject for my experiments over the years. I sat in a rocking chair in his living room; he lay on the floor in front of me. I read from the script in my hand, watching his face. When I saw him relax, I directed him to go to a past life. Wonder of wonders, he did. He began responding to my questions, telling me he was on a ship at sea. He told me how many sails the ship had; he spoke of the creaking of the wood and the sea surrounding the ship. The details were amazing. Strangely enough, in his present life he had joined the navy and spent many months at sea. A great deal of his free time was spent at the stern of the ship watching the water and sky, perfectly at peace. Also, he has built several models of old sailing vessels, complete with tiny sails. He has always been fascinated by the sea.

My point in telling you of my first experience in guiding someone through a regression is to let you know how very simple the procedure is. You can work with a friend; you can help your friend remember. So let's begin.

Begin with the script for relaxing your subject that is given in chapter 11. When working with another person (a subject) you need to respond according to the answers you are receiving. Frequently, if you are dealing with the subject's first regression, he or she will block impressions and will be vague about the surroundings. If that is the case, you can give the suggestion: "On the count of three, vivid impressions will come into your mind. You will know exactly where you are. One, two, three. Vivid impressions are coming in. What is your first thought or feeling?" Generally, the person you are working with will begin to respond at this point. Begin asking questions about the subject's surroundings, such as, "Tell me about the place you find yourself." If the subject is outside, ask about the environment. If inside, ask for details about the room or building. If the subject is slow to respond, keep in mind that he or she is in an altered state of consciousness. Ask your friend to look down and describe his or her footwear. And then inquire about clothing. People can usually give you a pretty full description of what they are wearing.

Once subjects are involved in the process, be aware that they have gone to this particular moment in time for a reason, even if what they are experiencing does not seem significant. I frequently give the suggestion, "Continue to allow events to unfold. Tell me what is happening." Given this instruction, they will generally do as instructed, and you will begin to understand what they are experiencing.

You can continue to move subjects forward in time by suggesting to them, "Move to an important event. On the count of three you will move to an important event, receiving vivid impressions. One, two, three. Where are you? What is happening?" Allow the story to unfold, giving them plenty of time to describe what they are experiencing.

Additional questions for details include the following:

1. What is your name? Hear it spoken: what are you called?
2. What country are you living in?
3. What are the names of the other people in this scene?
4. Go to your home. Describe it to me.
5. To discover who family members are, suggest: "Go forward in time to the evening meal. Tell me who is there. What is happening?"
6. The most important question you can ask is "How do you feel?" To go through a regression totally devoid of feelings is an exercise in futility. The more aware one becomes of the feelings involved in the experience, the more value it has.

If subjects become upset about events occurring in a past life, you can calm them by suggesting, "Detach emotionally from what is happening. Become an observer. You are not involved emotionally. Simply report to me what is happening, feeling very calm and emotionally detached from the events." We are finally learning in our society that our emotions do have value. It is important for each of us to be aware of our feelings, and to be able to express them. We have learned that if a friend is experiencing a severe loss, it is not wise to try to cheer them up, but to let them express their feelings. In a regression, as in real life, the most important thing that subjects can accomplish is to review past events and be aware of how they felt about those events. It is not wise to allow subjects to become too upset, so calming suggestions should be given. However, *under no circumstances* should you abruptly discontinue a session because your subjects have become upset. They will not be harmed. It is better to allow them to have the memory than for it to lie buried for centuries more. If your subjects indicate they would like to end the session, do so, after you have given them calming, reassuring suggestions.

The following is a transcript of a regression. I have included it so you can observe how I worked with the client, responding to what she was experiencing, moving her forward and back in time as needed, and urging her to let her memories come to the surface, in order to understand a present-life situation.

The client was a young woman. She came to me for weight loss. After our initial interview, I prepared a hypnosis tape designed for that goal. After working with the tape for several weeks, she saw no change in her weight.

When she came in for a third session, she told me, "I'm being blocked. I don't understand why this is happening. I've tried so many things, I was convinced this would help."

Reincarnation was not part of her belief system. From our previous conversations, I felt she might be willing to try a past-life regression, to seek an answer.

I suggested to her, "I know you don't believe in reincarnation, but I feel it might be of value to you to explore a possible past life tie to this block you are experiencing. Would you be willing to give it a try?"

"Right now?" she asked.

"Why not? Let's see what your mind will offer up to help you get beyond this block."

She was somewhat skeptical, but decided it would be worth trying.

She was already conditioned as a hypnosis subject, since she had been working with self-hypnosis for two weeks at this point. I briefly spoke about how she might receive impressions. I then guided her into an altered state of consciousness.

Jealousy and Death in the Past

[*Induce trance.*]

ELAINE: Your own mind will choose a lifetime to review that

will give you insight and understanding into your current circumstances, your current feeling about your need to protect yourself with some excess weight. Your mind will choose the past-life tie to these present circumstances.

[*Count backward from five to one, continuing to suggest that she will find the lifetime to review that will be helpful at this time.*]

ELAINE: Are you outside or inside? You have the ability to respond verbally to my questions.

JANE: Outside.

ELAINE: OK. What kind of place do you find yourself in? Where are you?

JANE: Mountains, hills . . . and orange-colored dirt.

ELAINE: All right, are you male or female?

JANE: Female.

ELAINE: How old are you?

JANE: In my mid-twenties.

ELAINE: What are you doing outside? Why are you where you are right now? What is the purpose of your being there?

JANE: It seems like I'm on a hill and I'm looking down over a valley . . . green trees . . . and there's a river or creek or something down there I can't see yet.

ELAINE: OK. How are you feeling?

JANE: Peaceful. . . . I have a long dress on.

ELAINE: OK. What is your name? What are you called?

JANE: Sally.

[*She chuckles slightly at the name.*]

ELAINE: Continue to allow events to unfold and tell me what transpires later in this particular day.

JANE: I'm going down the hill . . . the dirt. It's hard to keep my footing. I'm sliding sometimes. I can see that there's water down there. I'm almost down to the valley floor. Beautiful trees. It seems like a summer day. There's a breeze. I have an uneasy feeling. . . . Something's behind me.

[*She begins to breathe more deeply now, obviously becoming agitated.*]

ELAINE: What is happening?

JANE: I don't know. I can feel it in my back. It feels strange.

ELAINE: Do you feel that someone else is there?

JANE: Perhaps yes, there's someone sneaking up on me or something. Oh, I have a scared feeling.

ELAINE: What do you do?

JANE: I'm afraid to look around. I feel tearful. . . . I don't know why.

[*At this point her voice becomes emotional, as if she is about to cry. She cries. Her breathing becomes harder. She is obviously re-experiencing something that terrified her.*]

ELAINE: All right, you can allow these events to continue to unfold, but you will now be emotionally uninvolved. You will detach emotionally, feeling calm now, feeling very calm.

[*I continued to give calming instructions, until she became calm and in control. I instructed her to view the events as an observer. She is calm now.*]

ELAINE: Who is there? What is happening?

JANE: I'm not sure. It seems dark.

ELAINE: Is it night time now?

JANE: No, it just seems dark. I can't really tell.

ELAINE: Was someone else there? Had someone snuck up on you?

JANE: I feel like . . . Yes, that must have been it. I can't see. I can't tell if there was. I don't know.

ELAINE: I want you to go back to when that was happening. Allow events to unfold, remain emotionally detached, and just tell me what happened.

JANE: Something in my back . . . all I can see is . . . it feels like a hand. I don't know, it feels like a sharp object or something. It's hard not to be emotional, I don't know why.

ELAINE: OK. Did someone stab you? What happened?

JANE: Yes, it feels like the shoulder area, not high, but between my shoulder blades. Yes, there's a hand, I feel like there was a hand . . . grabbing my shoulder with one hand and . . . yes, stabbing me, or something, in my back.

ELAINE: OK. What was the result of that? Did you survive the attack?

JANE: I only have this feeling of seeing myself lying there . . . I don't know . . .

ELAINE: Let's move back in time, move back to before this event. Did you know your assailant? Did you know the person?

JANE: I don't think so.

ELAINE: Why did this happen?

JANE: The area . . . something to do with where I was . . . It was not what it seemed to be. It seemed like such a beautiful, tranquil place. Evil, it's something evil.

ELAINE: OK. I'll count from one to three and very vivid impressions will come into your mind. You will clearly understand exactly why that happened. One, two, three. Why did that happen?

JANE: Didn't like me.

ELAINE: The person who stabbed you didn't like you?

JANE: Didn't like me at all . . . hated me. Wanted to see me dead . . . jealousy . . . something . . .

ELAINE: Why was that person jealous?

JANE: Because of the way I was . . . something physical . . . the way I looked or something physical, I think. Jealousy.

ELAINE: Were you very attractive, very pretty?

JANE: I guess. I can't see myself to look at my face. I feel like I was taller and slender . . . light hair . . . but I can't see my face. I don't know. Jealousy is the only thing I can think of.

ELAINE: Why would this person go so far as to kill you? What was the root of this?

JANE: Now I can see the hand was feminine. I couldn't see it before. Her husband, something about her husband, someone she was emotionally involved with . . .

ELAINE: He found you attractive?

JANE: Yes . . . or I was involved with him and she wanted to be, or something. She had dark hair. A hat, she was wearing a hat, more like a bonnet. It was a knife, a horrible, huge knife. I didn't do anything to solicit this person, her husband or whoever . . . to want . . . to be attracted to me. I try to stay away from him. I don't want to be around him. I can't keep him from . . . It seems obvious to me that he is attracted, but I can't keep him from doing or being that way. He is very handsome, dark hair, dark eyes, somewhat muscular, athletic.

ELAINE: What is his name?

JANE: John.

ELAINE: And her name?

JANE: Rebecca.

[Jane's voice changes here, indicating she is beginning to understand the situation. It is becoming very real to her now.]

JANE: Oh, I see a child.

ELAINE: Who does the child belong to?

JANE: I think to her. It's not a very small child; it's eight or seven years old.

ELAINE: OK. Did she follow you to this place? Did she know you liked to go there?

JANE: I think so.

ELAINE: Did you sense or know before you felt her behind you that you were in any danger from her?

JANE: No, I knew he was attracted to me, and I was afraid that . . because she seemed someone to be afraid of . . . she seemed threatened. Although I didn't . . tried not to make her feel that way.

ELAINE: And were you very attractive?

JANE: I can't see my face.

ELAINE: But your body was very nice?

JANE: I was slender and somewhat tall. I was well endowed. I feel my skin was very fair. Makes me feel uneasy . . . before . . . I felt like she was glaring at me.

ELAINE: When did she see you?

JANE: It was them together mostly, not him alone.

ELAINE: So you had done nothing to draw him to you or attract him?

JANE: I don't think so. I could feel him looking at me, I knew he was interested. But it made me feel uneasy. I think he was married. I feel nervous.

ELAINE: Why are you feeling nervous now? What is happening?

JANE: I don't know. Maybe he's making advances. I don't know.

[Jane becomes upset again at this point, beginning to cry again. I give her calming suggestions, telling her to detach emotionally from what is happening.]

ELAINE: So he did make advances to you and that frightened you because you knew how angry or upset she would be?

JANE: I think it's because I knew he was married. I think I was attracted to him, but I knew he was married. Especially with the child, more guilt feelings. I felt guilty. I don't know why he chose me or came to me. But his child . . . How could he do that?

ELAINE: Is there a correlation in your present life? Is your need to be a little overweight and your not really approving of or liking yourself—is that a subconscious protection from this past life memory?

JANE: Yes, it must be. I feel calmer now.

ELAINE: OK. So there is a correlation here to what happened in that other time, which resulted in your death.

JANE: I was so frightened. There's no safe place.

ELAINE: So that has to do with your feeling insecure in this life?

JANE: Yes, it happened in a place where I felt safe and loved. And it happened because someone was attracted to me.

ELAINE: So it was your attractiveness and your innocence that brought this situation to you?

JANE: I think so.

ELAINE: OK. Let's move now into the highest levels of your own mind.

[One-to-five count given.]

ELAINE: What was the purpose or lesson learned in the lifetime you have just reviewed?

JANE: I can't get past the fear. I wished I wasn't so attractive then. It was something I couldn't fully deal with. I don't think I saw myself as being attractive, but I knew that I was.

ELAINE: What was the purpose? Why did you have that experience?

JANE: To teach me not to be so naive, not so trusting. I can trust, but not naively.

ELAINE: Anything else you need to be aware of now from your own higher mind? Any other guidance or instruction to help you in your present life?

JANE: No, nothing else now.

[*Instructions given to have total vivid recall of all she had experienced. I then suggested to her that she would totally and completely release at conscious and subconscious levels all negativity, all limitations from this experience.*]

ELAINE: You will bring forward the knowledge, wisdom, and understanding gained from that experience. You are now totally and completely free, secure within yourself, knowing that you can trust, but you need to trust with wisdom. You can allow yourself to be very attractive. You will trust in a healthy, positive way, and your being physically very attractive will not have any negative effects in your life. It will only enhance and create beauty and joy in your life. You will find after reviewing this experience that you are able to accept yourself, understand yourself, and be very nurturing with yourself. You are very open now to these positive suggestions. You totally release consciously and subconsciously all negative effects and limitations. These limitations are no longer appropriate or necessary. They are now released. You are in complete control of your body and mind. You give yourself permission at every level to be the perfect weight for you, to be physically attractive, to know it will enhance your life. You feel secure within yourself. You are aware of your personal power and use it in your life. You have opened the doors to your own subconscious mind. Any additional information you require will come to your conscious mind in the next few days in moments of quiet reflection or reverie, or perhaps in a dream. If there is additional information you need to be aware of, it will come to your conscious attention. You will take note of it and use it in your life. You are free now. You have released consciously and subconsciously all negative effects. You have understanding, and with that knowledge you have power. You will bring all these positive feelings and thoughts with you into your life now. On the count of five you'll open your eyes and be wide awake. You'll feel refreshed, calm, and very secure.

[*Count up given.*]

Notice that often the subject was not responding to the question I asked, but describing what she was becoming aware of. As I mentioned earlier, it is very important that you allow your subjects to tell their own story in their own way, as they are experiencing the past life.

Jane's first reaction when she came out of hypnosis was one of amazement. She could not believe that she had experienced all the emotional aspects of the regression. I asked her what her feelings were about the experience.

She replied, "I couldn't have made all that up. I couldn't have come to it so quickly, I didn't have time to think. It was just there."

"I know. Heaven only knows where it all comes from, but it is just there. We have to learn to trust what comes and know it has a purpose."

She sat for awhile, talking about her experience. There was an obvious impact. Even though she did not believe in reincarnation, her experience would be hard to ignore. I knew she had experienced a breakthrough in her weight-loss goal.

I called her the next afternoon to see how she was feeling about the regression. In our conversation she remarked, "I can feel there's a major difference in the mental block now. I'm feeling more positive. I feel like I will lose the weight now. I have a wonderful feeling of relief."

If you have ever sat with friends and talked with them about a problem they were dealing with, or held their hand as they wept and allowed them to speak of their grief, then you can guide another through a regression. As you can see from reading the transcript, my part in her drama was to calm her several times, and to ask the questions necessary for her story to unfold. A caring friend so often does the same thing.

Key Elements to a Successful Regression:

1. Give clear instructions about the purpose of the regression.
2. Start with easily answered questions, such as "Are you outside or inside?"
3. Listen attentively to the subject, responding to what they're saying, rather than asking preconceived questions.
4. If the subject goes to an event that is puzzling to you, direct them to move to the source of the situation.
5. If, after relating an incident, you are still unclear about why the event occurred, give the suggestion: "Go to the source of this situation, the root."
6. If the subject becomes upset, give the suggestion: "You will be calm now and emotionally detach from what is happening. Put this event on a view screen in your mind, detaching completely, and report what you see." Continue to give calming suggestions and the sugges-

tions to detach until they are calm. This may take a few minutes. Be patient.

7. If your subjects ever report that they feel they are spinning, this can be immediately counteracted with the suggestion: "Stabilize." This happens very rarely, but can easily be taken care of.

8. Do not rush your subject. If responses are slow, or if he or she is talking, do not interrupt with your comments or questions. Allow the story to unfold at your subject's pace.

9. Always end the session with the instructions: "You will have total, vivid recall of all you've experienced. You will release at conscious and subconscious levels all negativity, all limitations from this experience. You will bring forward into your current life the knowledge, wisdom, and understanding gained."

Also, suggest: "In the next few days, in moments of quiet reflection, reverie, or perhaps in a dream, if there is additional information you need to be aware of, it will come to your conscious mind. You will understand this information and use it in your life."

10. After giving the above suggestions, you can guide your subject into the highest levels of his or her mind. From that perspective you can ask: "What was the purpose of the life you just reviewed? Why did you choose to have those experiences?"

11. Also, from the perspective of the higher mind, you can ask the identity of any key people in the past life. Instruct your subject: "Look into the eyes of (name of person from past life). Is this someone you know in the present?" Amazingly enough your subject will know who it is. If not, it is probably someone the subject has not met, or will not meet this time.

12. Be aware that even though you have given a one-to-five count to awaken your subject, and your subject's

eyes are open, he or she is still in a light altered state and very suggestable. Say only positive, nurturing things. Do not make any negative statements or comments.

13. When your subject meets with death in a past life, do not be alarmed. Death is a calm, peaceful experience. It doesn't seem to matter if the person experiences a horrible death, or dies quietly in bed. It is always experienced as a release, a quiet, serene state. I've had many clients who, before their regression, had been afraid of dying. After experiencing their death in a regression they find their fear is now gone. They learn that whatever has happened to their physical body is no longer important, because they are now out of that body and free of all its limitations.

Solstice Regression

Buried in our subconscious are memories of powerful, ancient ceremonies. The winter and summer solstices have been celebrated throughout time. You may discover that you took part in this celebration. Perhaps you were in an Aztec temple, at Stonehenge, or Karnak. If you're interested, this could be an intriguing exploration. Some specific questions to ask are:

1. How were you dressed? How were the others dressed?
2. Your country or geographical location?
3. What are your surroundings (temple, large objects, etc.)?
4. Are there others participating with you?
5. What part did you have in the ceremony?
6. Was there an object or objects that represented the power of the ceremony?
7. What are your feelings about this special time? What does it mean to you, to your people?

8. What was the purpose or lesson learned?
9. How can this information be used in your life?

Atlantis or Lemuria Regressions

These are two ancient civilizations for which we have no historical data. However, they have been written and wondered about at great length. You may have been part of these ancient civilizations. Questions to ask:

1. Tell me about the place you live. What are the buildings like?
2. How are you dressed?
3. How do you communicate?
4. Do you use crystals for any special purposes?
5. How are records kept of your people's history?
6. If someone is ill, how are they cared for?
7. Did you have a unique skill or ability?
8. Could you relearn this skill or ability in your present life?
9. How does the life you are exploring relate to your present life and circumstances?

Skill or Ability Regressions

It is sometimes very helpful to know about past-life talents and abilities. If you are looking for a new direction, if you need to make a decision about a career change, or if you would like to explore a past-life connection to a current hobby or interest, a regression is an excellent tool. Direct your subjects to the lifetime in which their current interests or abilities were developed. If your subjects want information about a change of direction, direct them to the life that will give them insight and understanding into the changes occurring in their life. Questions to ask:

1. How do you spend the majority of your time?
2. Do others benefit from what you do?
3. How do you feel about your abilities?
4. Is this something you could easily relearn in the present?
5. Who is your mentor? Your teacher? Go to a significant time with this person.
6. How can you use this information in your current life?

Psychic Ability Regressions

Long ago, before our technologically-based, left-brain world was dominant, our intuition and psychic abilities were more finely developed. It is interesting to reconnect with that other time and to become aware of the benefits of being a little more in tune with the right brain. Instruct your subjects to go to the lifetime in which their psychic abilities were finely developed and used. Questions to ask:

1. What country or geographical location are you in?
2. Who is your primary teacher?
3. Go to a significant time with this person
4. How were you trained?
5. How was your training used to benefit others?
6. How do your people live? What is your life like?
7. Could you redevelop this ability in the present?
8. How can you use this information in your life now?

These are just a few suggestions. Obviously, you will need to respond to what your subject is telling you. The above questions are only suggestions, to give you some idea of the explorations that are possible.

Use discretion when you work with another person. The information you become privy to is confidential and should not be shared with others without permission.

You may find as you work with regressive hypnosis that you

are seeing everything your subject sees. You may know what they are experiencing. If this happens, it is an indication of your own psychic abilities. You are very sensitive and able to sense another's feelings. Do not be alarmed. This ability is a gift.

Use this tool wisely. It will help you and whoever you work with immensely. Be prepared to be constantly amazed at the stories you hear. They will never be the same. Some will be tedious to listen to, others will make you lean forward on your chair, wanting to hear more. The amazing thing about our minds is that there always is more than we can possibly imagine. Enjoy the journey.

CHAPTER 13

Regression Transcripts to Teach You

The most difficult aspect of guiding someone through a past life regression is learning to listen carefully to what they are experiencing and asking appropriate questions. The main reason most past-life guides experience difficulty is because they are too busy thinking about what they are going to say and not truly listening to the subject. Your natural curiosity will lead you to ask the best questions. Think of it this way: if a friend of yours went on an exciting trip and met interesting new people, you would ask questions as your friend related the adventure. Guiding a friend through a past life is very much the same. But because the individual is in a trance, you will need to ask more questions to learn about his or her experience. You will not be overwhelmed if you will think of the subject as simply telling a story giving you the opportunity to ask questions and learn something new.

Another difficulty may be your subject's inability to allow impressions to come through. It's frustrating when you ask someone, "Where are you, outside or inside?" and they respond with, "I don't see anything." While conducting workshops teaching people these techniques, I've noticed that the minute there is a block, the students are ready to bring their subjects out of hypnosis and give up. Because I have a lot of experience with clients, I know it's possible for anyone to allow themselves to receive impressions. I simply signal the students to persevere in their attempts to guide their subjects through a regression. Almost without fail they are able to do so, if they will continue working with their subjects.

The following transcripts are included to help you with the process of guiding another through a past life. Read them carefully, noting the instructions. Keep in mind you are trying to obtain information that will be useful and helpful to the person you are working with.

The first transcript is an excellent example of someone who blocked impressions initially, not allowing herself to receive anything at all. This often happens when the subject is very analytical. In this particular case the subject was at a difficult time in her life, needing to decide whether to continue her marriage. She was a woman in her mid-forties, attractive, bright, and articulate. Her life looked like a storybook from the outside. She was attending school and lived very comfortably, but there was no love in her marriage. She wanted to explore a possible past-life tie with her husband that would help her understand their relationship and her feelings. There are, of course, no easy answers. But once again, knowledge is power, and understanding why you find yourself in a particular set of circumstances can help you make difficult decisions.

Very often when subjects really needs answers, they will be difficult to guide into a past life, because subconsciously they do not want to know the answers. Consequently they will have difficulty allowing themselves to receive information from a past life. If you work with regressive hypnosis you will inevitably deal with people who are blocking impressions. You can see how I worked with this woman, refusing to give up. If you keep asking and gently guiding, subjects generally will allow themselves to receive impressions.

During our conversation before the regression, this woman asked if she could also explore her feelings about "walking in a garden just before sunset, when the shadows fall a certain way." I made a note of this request before we began. At the end of the first regression, because she did not seem overly tired from her experience, I guided her to explore the second lifetime. The second regression gave her even more insight into her present circumstances, because that past life was affecting her present life.

Choices and Risks

[*Trance induced.*]

ELAINE: You will choose a lifetime that has the most influence on your relationship with the man you know now as John, who is your husband. You will allow your own mind to choose a lifetime to review that has the strongest affect on your current feelings for, and your relationship with, the person you know now as John.

[*Be very specific with your suggestions about the life your subject wants to explore.*]

Here I used a backward count from five to one, continuing to suggest she would choose a lifetime to explore with the person she knows now as John.

ELAINE: On the next count you will be in another time and place, trusting the thoughts and feelings that come to you. . . . Are you outside or inside? Where do you find yourself?

[*This is the best question to ask initially because it allows your subject to easily begin receiving impressions. If you ask something more complicated, you will confuse your subject and make it difficult for them to begin.*]

BARBARA: I don't know.

ELAINE: Trusting yourself completely now, what is your first thought or feeling? Where are you?

[*Usually, this amount of reinforcement will help your subject get beyond the block they are experiencing. As you can see, it did not help her.*]

BARBARA: I'm just not getting anything.

ELAINE: Don't try, no effort is involved, no effort at all, relax even further now. Let your first thought or feeling come, without any conscious effort, without preconceived ideas. Simply allow yourself to float and drift. Going deeper and deeper into relaxation. So relaxed, so at ease, drifting now even deeper and deeper. All cares and concerns simply floating away, drifting into deeper, more peaceful levels of consciousness. Your entire body is feeling so relaxed and so at ease, your mind is free, your body is relaxed, drifting deeper and deeper now. You will allow yourself to create a fantasy situation, to create another time and place in which you knew the man you know now as John. You will allow yourself to simply create, to fantasize another time and place in which you lived. We will go to that time and place now, trusting completely, giving yourself permission to imagine, to trust those images. Moving back in time now. Number three—moving back in time, way, way back in time to another time and place; number two—moving back in time, trusting completely; number one—you're there now. Tell me if you're outside or inside, trusting completely.

[Because my client's voice did not sound relaxed at all, I took the time to deepen her trance. It is important to stay tuned to your subject, to suggest they relax further if needed.]

BARBARA: I'm just not getting anything.

ELAINE: What you're doing is you're thinking, you're using your conscious mind, and you're thinking in a linear fashion. You have to give yourself permission now to fantasize and imagine. You can move into that creative part of your own mind now that is filled with stories. I want you now to make up a story. Make up a story of another time and place. I want you to create a fantasy, and you will be part of that fantasy. You are able to do this, it comes easily and effortlessly to you. I will count backward from three to one and you will create a story of another time and place. Number three—moving back, trusting completely; number two—moving to another time and place with John. You are now there. Create this in your mind now. Where are you?

[*Because she continued to block impressions, I then suggested she would "fantasize" another time and place. This allowed her to go beyond her conscious thinking and begin receiving impressions.*]

BARBARA: It looks like I'm outside somewhere.

ELAINE: Are you male or female?

BARBARA: I see a male . . . standing by a tree.

ELAINE: What is this place like?

BARBARA: It looks like it's just in a field and he's standing by a tree. He looks like he's wearing brown boots and white tights and a kind of tunic. A reddish tunic.

ELAINE: What is he doing there?

BARBARA: It looks like he just got off a horse.

ELAINE: So he's been riding. Is anyone with him?

BARBARA: No, he looks like he's alone.

ELAINE: Why is he there? What's the purpose of his being there?

BARBARA: I think he's hunting.

ELAINE: Continue to allow events to unfold and tell me what transpires next.

BARBARA: Looks like he's getting back on again and riding somewhere very swiftly. I think he has a dog. I think he's hunting pheasants or something.

ELAINE: All right, continue to allow events to unfold, and tell me what happens now.

BARBARA: I think he shot a pheasant and he's picking it up. He's happy he has it. I think he's just doing this for fun, for leisure.

ELAINE: How old is he?

BARBARA: He looks like he's in his thirties.

ELAINE: What happens next?

BARBARA: He's riding back to the castle. There's a moat. . . . He's riding over it. There's someone waiting for him . . . a woman. He drops the birds at her feet and he stomps off. He stomps off, he doesn't say very much to her. I think the woman is me.

[*Because she had been blocking impressions, her first images are of her husband from that time. This was another way for her own subconscious to block what was happening. I made no comment about this, but simply began directing my questions to the woman she then saw herself as.*]

ELAINE: How do you feel when he returns?

BARBARA: I was waiting for him, I must have been looking for him. He threw the birds down right at my feet as if he didn't really care. I'm running after him. It's almost as if he's mad at me, he's ignoring me.

ELAINE: What's the source of his displeasure or anger? Move back in time so you can understand the source of his displeasure. Three, two, one. What is happening?

[*You can move your subject back in time to clarify a present situation. Going back in time will help your subject receive more details about what is happening.*]

BARBARA: He looks like he's yelling at me over dinner or something. He's unhappy about something. He's just a very . . . he's uptight.

ELAINE: How do you deal with his anger or frustration?

BARBARA: I don't argue back. He's raging on and on about something. I can't tell what he's so mad about.

ELAINE: What do you think and feel as he rages on and on? What are your own thought processes and feelings?

[*Always be sure to ask about the feelings your subject is experiencing. Their feelings are an important key to the present situation.*]

BARBARA: That he's doing it just to pick on me. We're at a very long table in a very cold hall. Only two of us there. I think there are some servants standing nearby, but his voice is echoing in the hall.

ELAINE: Do you feel humiliated or hurt?

BARBARA: I feel like it's a normal part of our married life, that he just picks on me.

ELAINE: Let's move back in time, once again, to the time of your first meeting with him. Three, two, one. Where are you now? What is happening?

[*I feel it's important for her to explore the beginning of this relationship, and so direct her to move back in time to their first meeting.*]

BARBARA: He's in a very expensive outfit. He's in white tights again, only the tunic has silver and gold on it, jewels. He seems to be blond. I don't think he was blond before, but he is now.

ELAINE: What's the occasion of your meeting, why are you meeting?

BARBARA: Something to do with falcons . . . a falcon hunt.

ELAINE: How do you feel when you see him and meet him?

BARBARA: I really have no feelings at all. I don't love him and I don't hate him. And I'm in a blue gown. I just have no feelings for him one way or other. I'm a little afraid.

ELAINE: Why are you afraid?

BARBARA: He seems to be a king or something. I just think I'm a very passive person and he's not . . .

ELAINE: Would marrying him form an important alliance for your family?

BARBARA: I think I was sent there to marry him. I don't love him at all. I think I was sent there. In fact I'm picking up that I'm not very happy.

ELAINE: What happens? How do you deal with this unhappiness?

[*At this point the subject began wiping tears from her cheeks. She was getting in touch with her feelings surrounding these circumstances. Be certain to ask your subjects about their feelings. It was not necessary to give suggestions to Barbara to detach emotionally because she was not terribly upset. She remained in a somewhat light trance through the regression.*]

BARBARA: I can't do anything. I have to be there. . . . and I really don't want to be there. I don't want to marry him.

ELAINE: Does he know how you feel?

BARBARA: He doesn't care. It's like he doesn't even see me as a person. He just thinks: she's to be my wife and bear my children. There's no love at all.

ELAINE: And how do you feel?

BARBARA: I don't like that at all.

ELAINE: Do you try to dissuade your family from the marriage? Is this possible?

BARBARA: No. I did not try at all.

ELAINE: Your family is not present for the wedding?

BARBARA: It's not a wedding. I'm just there. It's a hunt or some other occasion. It seems like he has a falcon or something.

ELAINE: Let's move forward now to the time when you become his wife. One, two, three. Where are you now, what is happening?

[As you can see I asked many questions to fill in the details of what was happening. It is necessary to ask questions so that both you and your subject can understand what is happening.]

BARBARA: I'm sitting on a throne next to him. And I'm feeling intimidated, like I don't want to be there. I wonder, why am I doing this? Why do I have to do this?

ELAINE: What happens?

BARBARA: He's not paying any attention to me. He's talking with someone else. I'm looking straight ahead. He looks bored almost, as if he's thinking, let's just get this whole thing over with.

ELAINE: And then what happens?

BARBARA: He gets off the throne and he reaches out and I accept his hand and I step down. We're walking down a red velvet runner. There are people in the hall. They're laughing and having fun, rejoicing about the union, and I just don't want to be there.

ELAINE: Continue to allow events to unfold, tell me about your first days and weeks as his wife. How do you feel?

BARBARA: He's gone. I'm left on my own, and I like to take

a walk out beyond the castle because it's quiet. But I'm still very unhappy.

ELAINE: Do you have a confidant, or friend, anyone for you to talk with?

BARBARA: There's no one. I'm far, far away from everyone. [Again her voice begins to become emotional. Tears run down her cheeks freely.]

ELAINE: You're totally at his mercy then?

BARBARA: Yes.

ELAINE: You're very unhappy and there's nothing you can do? You have no options or choices?

BARBARA: Yes.

ELAINE: Move forward to a significant or clarifying event. Where are you?

BARBARA: I can't see anything.

ELAINE: See yourself walking outside the castle walls again.

[*If your subject begins to block impressions during a regression, describe the immediately preceding scene and ask the subject to continue from there.*]

BARBARA: I want to kill myself.

ELAINE: You're feeling that desolate, that abandoned? Does he have any idea how you feel?

BARBARA: No. I don't talk to him. It's . . . I don't talk.

ELAINE: Continue now to allow events to unfold. How do you deal with these strong feelings about taking your own life?

BARBARA: It makes me feel as if I have something to do to get me out of the situation. It makes me feel better.

ELAINE: Do you decide to act on those feelings?

BARBARA: I'm afraid to.

ELAINE: What is the source of your fear? Is it a religious reason?

BARBARA: No, I like life. It's beautiful outside away from the awful grey castle. And when I'm out here alone I feel more peaceful. More content. Even though it's a damp, awful climate.

ELAINE: What country are you in?

BARBARA: I think I'm in England.

ELAINE: What year is it?

BARBARA: I think it's the 1600s. 1666.

ELAINE: Continue to allow events to unfold. Tell me what happens next.

BARBARA: I can't see anything.

[*She is blocking again. I counteract this with a suggestion about going to a specific event.*]

ELAINE: Go forward to a specific event with your husband, to something that occurs between the two of you. One, two, three. Where are you? What is happening?

BARBARA: I think I'm older. It looks like I have grey hair, and I'm still in that awful castle. I've gotten stronger. We're in the dining room. That damp, ugly dining room with that awful, ugly wooden table. Everything is so . . . nothing is fine. There are no fine dishes. Everything's coarse and heavy. The stone floor . . . there's no one in the room but me. I think I'm dead.

ELAINE: How did you become stronger? You said you were feeling stronger, feeling stronger within yourself. How did this happen?

BARBARA: I think he died.

ELAINE: And that gave you more personal freedom?

BARBARA: I think it did. I think I have children. I think I have a son. Yes, I have one son.

ELAINE: Is he there with you in the dining hall?

BARBARA: He just walked in. And I love my son. And he's calling me mother.

ELAINE: What is his name? What do you call him?

BARBARA: Ralph . . . not Ralph, but something with an *R* . . . Rolf.

ELAINE: He brings you happiness?

BARBARA: I'm very proud of him. I feel happy.

ELAINE: How long has your husband been dead?

BARBARA: Twenty years.

ELAINE: Has your son taken over his father's position? Does he govern or carry on with his father's duties?

BARBARA: He's very young, he's only nineteen or twenty. He's starting to do that. I think someone else has been in charge for a long time.

ELAINE: I want you to go back and be aware of how your husband died and be aware of the circumstances surrounding his death. Three, two, one. Where are you now? What is happening?

BARBARA: I was told he died in battle. Someone threw a spear through his chest.

ELAINE: How did you feel when you received this news?

BARBARA: Sad, but relieved. There was never any love between us. I feel sad because I feel I've lost a companion even though he was not a good one. But then I feel relieved that he's gone.

ELAINE: And your life becomes more peaceful after his death?

BARBARA: Yes. I have a son, he's a little baby. He's a very curly-haired blond, a pretty little baby. I'm very happy with this little baby.

ELAINE: Move forward in time again now to when your son walked into the dining hall and you were feeling happy. One, two, three. What is happening?

[*I feel we've explored her husband's death enough at this point and move her forward again in time to the event she described before I moved her back in time.*]

BARBARA: He's happy about something . . . or he's discussing what he's done. I think he's hunting. I think that's all they did for leisure, they hunted. He's coming back from a hunt and he has pheasant. He's happy about that.

ELAINE: Does he live there at the castle with you?

BARBARA: Yes, he does.

ELAINE: Tell me about the castle. How does it look?

BARBARA: It's very large. It has a moat around it. It's very cold and damp and ugly. All the activity seemed to take place in the dining room.

ELAINE: Move forward to the next significant or important event that occurs.

[*This is the best suggestion to move your subject ahead in time to events that are important for them to remember.*]

BARBARA: It's my death. I see myself . . . I always wore blue. Oh, I hate that color. It's a light blue and I've got long grey hair. I'm in a hall in the castle. I'm just dead.

ELAINE: Is anyone there with you?

BARBARA: There's not a lot of people. There's my son and he's about twenty-eight. And he's very sad, and there's maybe five or six people just milling around. It's as though I'm looking at the scene saying, "Rolf, I'm sorry I died."

ELAINE: Why do you feel sorry about your death?

BARBARA: I don't know why.

ELAINE: You're going to have total, vivid recall of all you've experienced. We're going to move once again in time now to another time and another place. We will explore the flashes you've had in this life about walking in a garden, in a very green setting, just before sunset, when the shadows fall a certain way. We will explore the feeling you get, the feeling about wondering why. I will count backward from three to one, and you will be in this other time and place. You will know exactly what is happening. Three, two, one. Where are you now? What is happening?

[*After exploring one lifetime, you can guide your subject to another life with similar suggestions. Before this session began my client had asked me to find out the meaning of feelings. Take note of names and the place so that at the end of the entire session you can ask questions about the lesson learned and the people involved.*]

BARBARA: A stone building. There seems to be a hill. I'm with a man. He's Spanish and he's laughing. I'm with him and I am laughing. We're happy. I think we're going to be married.

ELAINE: What country are you in?

BARBARA: Spain.

ELAINE: What is the year?

BARBARA: It seems to be the 1800s. I think 1840. And he is very happy. He's laughing and hugging me. But I seem to be a cold person. I'm happy that he loves me, but I don't seem to be able to have the capacity to love him as much as he loves me. Even though I'm happy. I think he senses this unhappiness in me.

ELAINE: Do you marry him?

BARBARA: I think I do.

ELAINE: What is his name? What is he called?

BARBARA: I think his name is Enrique.

ELAINE: Move forward after your marriage and tell me about your life with him after your marriage.

BARBARA: It's a very good marriage. I see him as an old man. He's still very kind and easy-going. He's holding my hand. We seem to be older. I am very contented with him. I think there's a big family. We've had a large family. He is a very happy person. But for some reason I'm not that happy a person. I came into this life and I'm feeling sad about something, I don't know what.

ELAINE: Let's go back in time to the source of the sadness. Three, two, one. What is happening?

BARBARA: I'm back at that castle.

ELAINE: What is the source of the sadness?

BARBARA: It seems to be centered around the fact that I don't really want to marry him. That I'm feeling that I'm not married to him yet and I want to do anything I can to stop this marriage. And why I've carried this unhappiness and kept it with me in a lifetime I don't . . . because I feel very content around Enrique. He's a very good man. He has always loved me. I don't know why I was born an unhappy person.

ELAINE: Continue to explore your relationship and marriage with Enrique. Tell me about your life with him.

[*She has gone back to the previous regression, so I bring her forward again with specific instructions about what she had just been telling me. Obviously, these two lives are intertwined and both are affecting her now.*]

BARBARA: He's very easy to get along with. He never yells. He seems to accept life as it comes to him. He's a large landowner. He loves his children. He loves his grandchildren. And I'm amazed he's such a peaceful, contented man.

ELAINE: And what are your feelings about the relationship and your life with him?

BARBARA: I'm very content with him. I love him. I guess I'm deeply in love with him. There don't seem to have been too many problems in that lifetime.

ELAINE: Go to the last day of that lifetime, the very last day. Tell me where you are and what is happening.

BARBARA: I'm very sick and I'm old. I want to go back and find Enrique. I'm tired of living. It's time to die. I want to be buried with my husband. I don't like it that I've lived so long.

ELAINE: Let go of this for now. You will have total, vivid recall of all you've experienced. We're going to move into the highest levels of your own mind.

[*Give instructions and a one-to-five count, moving her into the highest levels of her mind.*]

ELAINE: From this perspective I want you to be aware of the purpose or lesson learned in the first lifetime you reviewed when you lived in the castle.

[*When giving instructions at the end of a regression where more than one lifetime has been explored, be specific as to which lifetime you are referring to.*]

BARBARA: To learn to fight back. To stand up for what I

believe in. I should have left. I should never have stayed. I should have run away. I didn't. My son made up for all the bad in that life. But I should have stood up to my husband.

ELAINE: Look in your husband's eyes from that life. Tell me if he is someone you know in the present?

BARBARA: Yes it is.

ELAINE: Look into the eyes of your son. Is he someone you know now?

BARBARA: He could possibly be my daughter.

ELAINE: In the second lifetime in Spain, what was the purpose, the lesson learned?

BARBARA: To learn to love my husband. To be able to love and not let the experience with my first husband destroy me, although it definitely affected my life. I've got to learn how to love, to give my love to a man.

ELAINE: What do you need to change about the way you love, the way you are in a relationship?

BARBARA: I need to learn to trust more. I need to find someone that I can trust. I cannot trust John.

[*I am asking her questions to help her see the correlation between her past life and her present situation. The more questions you ask, the greater opportunity for your subject to understand and use the information in the present.*]

ELAINE: Look in Enrique's eyes and tell me if he is someone you know now?

BARBARA: He's someone I haven't met, but he reminds me very much of an artist whose work I admire.

ELAINE: What other guidance or information do you need from your own higher mind that will assist you at this time?

BARBARA: I would like to go back and find Enrique.

ELAINE: How can you use the information you've received to help yourself in your current life and circumstances?

BARBARA: I need to get away. I cannot repeat the same mistake I made. I need to learn how to be happy. I need to learn how to work, to love another man. I cannot . . . it does me no good to have this coldness towards men.

ELAINE: What is the first thing you can do to help yourself get over this coldness you feel toward men? What specific thing can you do?

BARBARA: It's obvious I should leave John. Maybe I thought he would be different. I don't know why I chose him again. Why would I choose him again if I was so unhappy?

ELAINE: Possibly to give you both an opportunity to be warmer with each other, to show concern, to care.

BARBARA: But we haven't.

ELAINE: Anything else now that you need to be aware of that would be helpful?

BARBARA: I need to learn to stand up for what I believe in. Also, when I'm angry, not to hold it inside of me. To release it so that I don't go from life to life carrying this with me. I need to stop thinking that I cannot do anything for myself, when I can.

ELAINE: Anything else?

BARBARA: I need to find someone who is happy. I would like to find Enrique. He was happy and he made me happy. I guess I'm sad that I didn't choose him. I think it would be very hard to get back to him if I did not choose him. I find that very sad.

ELAINE: And if you choose to release this relationship, your present marriage, will you heal that part of yourself that feels this pain?

BARBARA: Yes. Yes, I will go on. I will understand there is nothing I can do to change him. It's not my fault that he is just that kind of person. I cannot waste a lot of my life trying to prove this. I cannot change him. And it's not my fault that he is the way he is.

ELAINE: Anything else?

BARBARA: No.

[*When your subject announces there is nothing else to be aware of at this time, the regression has ended. Make certain you have given them every opportunity to receive insight from their own mind.*]

ELAINE: You're going to have total recall of all you've experienced. In the next few days, in moments of quiet reflection, in reverie, perhaps in a dream, if there is additional information that will be helpful to you, that will give you a sense of purpose and strength and inner awareness, that information will come to your conscious mind. You will acknowledge this information and use it in your life. You are using your mind to gain insight and understanding into your life and circumstances. You have opened the door to your own subconscious mind. You now allow that part of yourself to guide and direct you in your life. You bring forward the knowledge, wisdom, and understanding gained from these experiences, and you totally release any negativity, any limitations in your present life. [*Subject given instructions to return to normal levels of consciousness. Because subjects are in an altered state of consciousness, they are more susceptible to positive suggestions. It is good to end a session with positive, helpful suggestions based on the past life they have explored.*]

This regression was like so many others experienced by women I've worked with. We live in a time of great opportunity for women. These opportunities sometimes feel oppressive. In our society we're still programmed to believe that our happiness will come from a marriage, financial ease, children, a nice house in suburbia. We are finding that this prescribed formula does not always bring joy into our lives. We are beginning to awaken to our inner selves, to the part we need to play in our own lives to achieve happiness and balance. Is this woman's task in the present to take responsibility for her life? Was her decision to marry her husband in this life based on the security she knew life with him would offer, based on that past life in England in the 1600s? Did she choose not to be with Enrique because a part of her needed to deal with making choices in this life? In the 1600s she had few choices available to her. The only choice she was able to come up with was suicide. In the present she has many choices, but they involve risks that she couldn't take in that other time, but can now if she chooses to. She cannot change her husband or take responsibility for the way he is. He is on his own path, with his own learning to do.

There are no easy answers. Each of us must spend time contemplating our life, must feel our own pain and make our own decisions. Every day we stand at a crossroad. Every day there are choices to be made. Our answers are within us. We must learn to trust our inner guidance.

This next transcript relates the regression of another woman who was experiencing difficulty in her marriage. She had two loves, her husband and dancing. She had been teaching and performing Middle Eastern dancing (belly dancing) for the past ten years. Because of her husband's jealousy her performing had been restricted. At one point, she had given up her dancing for four years because her husband felt it was inappropriate for his wife. During that four years she had been completely miserable and had decided to resume dancing publicly no matter what the consequences. She was completely confused by her husband's reaction. The consequences were predictable. Her husband became even more angry when she resumed dancing. Intuitively she felt there was more to the problem than there appeared to be. She never danced in cabarets. Her costumes were not skimpy. She did everything she could to assure him that she loved him and wanted to be with him, but needed to dance.

When she came in for her appointment we talked about the turmoil in her life. She said her home was like an armed camp, with the tension barely tolerable. I felt, as she did, that there was definitely a past-life tie to the problem. As you'll see in the transcript, dancing has always been very important to her, and the conflict began centuries ago.

An Independent Woman

[*Trance induced.*]

ELAINE: Go to the lifetime that will provide you with insight and understanding about the conflict in your life with your husband and your dancing. We will go back to another time and place that will explain this situation to you so that you will understand more fully the conflict in your life now over your dancing.

[*Give one-to-five count to guide her to the past life.*]

ELAINE: Are you outside or inside? Where do you find yourself?

MARJORIE: Half and half, but mostly inside.

ELAINE: What do you mean outside and inside? What do you mean?

[*If you don't understand the answer to your question, you can ask for clarification. Your subject will readily comply.*]

MARJORIE: I'm standing in a tent, the front is completely open. I'm leaning on the post in the middle.

ELAINE: Are you male or female?

MARJORIE: Female.

ELAINE: Describe this place to me.

MARJORIE: The tent is striped, it's green and yellow. There are gourds and things that we've tied to the beams. When I look out I see the desert, and I know behind me is a street with other tents and buildings on it. But we want to face away from the town.

ELAINE: What is the significance of the gourds and things tied to the tent?

MARJORIE: We use them for grains. We use them to go to the well for water. They're mostly for food.

ELAINE: How are you dressed? What are you wearing?

MARJORIE: I'm wearing a beige-colored loose robe. It's plain. I have a woven belt on. That's all.

ELAINE: How old are you?

MARJORIE: I'm forty.

ELAINE: What is your name, hear it spoken?

[*Notice that when I ask a question of the subject, I say "What is your name?" not "Can you tell me your name?" If you ask your subjects if they can tell you, you bring them into their left, linear brain, and they have to decide if they* can *tell you, which creates confusion.*]

MARJORIE: Akasha.

ELAINE: Akasha?

MARJORIE: Yes, it means "golden lamp."

ELAINE: Is there anyone else in the tent with you?

MARJORIE: No, I'm waiting for my girls to come home.

ELAINE: Are these your daughters?

MARJORIE: I don't have any children. I never did.

ELAINE: Who are the girls you are waiting for?

MARJORIE: They're girls who are prostitutes. Two are orphans. Three of them went to find some material. They went to a shop.

ELAINE: How do you feel about them?

MARJORIE: I love them. They're my family.

ELAINE: Move forward in time to when the girls arrive home. One, two, three. What is happening now?

MARJORIE: They found some beautiful gold material. It's a beautiful color, yellow with a gold border. They're unrolling it.

ELAINE: What will this fabric be used for?

MARJORIE: For a costume, to dance in.

ELAINE: What is your relationship with these girls? Do they live with you in this tent?

MARJORIE: Yes, we all live here.

ELAINE: How long have you lived together?

MARJORIE: Oh, probably ten years, but sometimes the girls will leave and new girls will come. Some have stayed with me from the beginning.

ELAINE: Go back in time to what you refer to as the beginning. Move back to that time now. Three, two, one. What is happening?

MARJORIE: I have just finished dancing in a cabaret. I'm very tired. I look at myself and I know I can't do it much longer. I'm thirty and I'm getting lines under my eyes. I'm too thin. I can't dance much longer. They want younger, prettier women. I don't know how much longer I will get money from the men. I have to find some other way to survive. I don't want to be a prostitute.

ELAINE: Is being a prostitute the only alternative to you? Is there something else you could do?

MARJORIE: I don't know of anything. If you're not married there is no way to live.

ELAINE: You don't have a husband?

MARJORIE: I ran away from him.

ELAINE: Let's move back in time to the time you ran away from your husband. Three, two, one. What is happening?

MARJORIE: I'm at the house I lived in when I was married. He's very angry. He's talking about Mohammed and the ethics of women. Mohammed is founding a new religion. He says that women have to be completely covered in front of anyone other than a male relative. I don't want to live that way. I belong to the old religion. I just can't live that way.

ELAINE: What is the old religion called?

MARJORIE: Khaliran.

ELAINE: What does that mean?

MARJORIE: The ways of the earth. It's a belief in gods and demons. The gods and the demons keep the earth in balance.

ELAINE: How do you deal with this conflict?

[If your subject is obviously experiencing a conflict about what is happening, ask how he or she resolved the conflict. This question always elicits further insight.]

MARJORIE: I defy him. He says I'm bringing shame on the family. I bring shame to him because I haven't had any children.

ELAINE: He feels you've brought shame on the family because you haven't had any children. And what else?

MARJORIE: Because I take my veil off my face sometimes when I'm out.

ELAINE: What country are you living in?

MARJORIE: Arabia.

ELAINE: What is your husband's name? Hear it spoken.

MARJORIE: Something like "Koranale."

[If your subject introduces a new person in response to your questions, ask who that person is. Make a note of it so you can ask at the end of the regression if this is someone known in the present.]

ELAINE: What do you decide to do? How will you resolve this conflict?

MARJORIE: I will run away.

ELAINE: Where will you go?

MARJORIE: I don't care. I think about just running away into the desert, or maybe to a different town.

ELAINE: Allow events to unfold and tell me what transpires.

MARJORIE: I take my jewelry. All of it. I have a lot. I leave the house in the middle of the night and I walk to a different town. It takes several days. When I'm there I find a room. I rent a room above a shop. I sell my jewelry a little at a time. I look for someone who will pay me to work. All the work is done by the wives of the shopowners. Everyone is suspicious of me. They wonder if I'm married and where my husband is. They sense something is wrong and they don't want to be involved. I'm getting discouraged.

[My subject is speaking very slowly throughout the regression. I wait and do not assume a pause indicates she is through speaking.

Allow enough time to let events unfold to the inner eye. Your subject will give you more information. Watch your subject's breathing, which becomes more pronounced as more is remembered. If you observe rapid eye movement, then you know the subject is still watching his or her internal movie. Allow plenty of time for the subject to tell you what is happening. Be patient.]

ELAINE: What do you decide to do?

MARJORIE: One night I see a girl dancing and I see the men throwing money to her or putting money in the little bag on her belt. She's wearing a lot of coins. I know that I can dance because I've danced all my life. I learned to dance from my mother. All women learn to dance from their mothers. Men and women separate at celebrations. We women danced at marriages and births and when girls entered puberty. Dancing was part of my life. I can dance better than the girl I'm watching. My style is better. I think it's better. So I go to a cabaret that is open to the street on two sides and I start to dance close by it. Some of the men start to watch, and they like it. I like to dance because I feel I have control. I don't feel like a victim. I feel like I'm in control. They throw coins in my direction. I gather them up and go home and count them.

ELAINE: How do you feel about this new life you've created for yourself?

MARJORIE: I'm surprised. I start thinking this might be a good thing.

ELAINE: Continue to allow events to unfold and tell me what happens now.

[This is a good suggestion to use to prompt more information from your subject.]

MARJORIE: I save some of the money that I'm getting to make a pretty dress. I have a little of my jewelry left. I get braver. I start moving deeper into the street cabarets. The owners encourage me. They don't throw me out. One asks me to come every night, so I do. I don't make a lot of money, but I make enough to survive, enough to have a couple of pretty dresses. During the day I veil my face because I don't want to be recognized by the men, and I don't want the women to be angry with me.

ELAINE: Let's move forward in time to a significant event. One, two, three. Where are you? What is happening?

MARJORIE: I'm at the point where I've decided I can't continue to dance. I'm getting old and I don't feel good. I feel weak. It's hard to dance all night like this. I think something's wrong. I'm walking home and I see prostitutes in the street . . . in the corner, in the shadows. I go up to one and ask if she wants to live some other way. She says, "I can't do anything. What else can I do?" So I take her to my room that night. I want to see what she's like before I make an offer. We just talk. I let her sleep there. I give her some food. I say, "I could teach you to dance. You could give me a little of the money you make every night, just a little." She says, "Well, maybe." So I show her some things. She says she's willing to try.

ELAINE: So you begin to teach her to dance?

MARJORIE: Yes, and I let her try on my dresses and that sells her more than anything. She likes to wear them.

ELAINE: Continue to allow events to unfold. What happens now?

MARJORIE: She stays with me, and after a few weeks I take her with me to work at night. I let her go first. The men like her. She has a lot to learn, but the men like her. She's excited, because it is such an easy way to get money. She says she wants to get even better, and she's happy about it. I let her do most of the dancing that night. I dance towards the end of the evening, and then we go home. Later we start to think about . . . she has a friend who would like to join us. We can't take any more now. It's too hot and it's getting stuffy in this small room. So we buy fabric and get olive branches, and we make an open-air tent on the outskirts out of the town. We talk about more girls maybe, because then we would be more secure. The next girl we get is a little girl about ten.

ELAINE: Where is this little girl's family?

MARJORIE: She's an orphan.

ELAINE: There's no one to care for her?

MARJORIE: No, she's been living on the streets. The prostitutes have been sharing a little food with her here and there. She just sleeps in alleys, so we take her in.

ELAINE: Then what happens? Continue to allow this to unfold.

MARJORIE: We go on like this for a long time. One girl has a baby. I like to take care of it. I stay with the baby while they go off and do their dancing. They go to other parts of the town. I take care of the baby and I really like it. I don't dance anymore.

ELAINE: What is the name of this town? Where are you?

MARJORIE: Caldar.

ELAINE: And what is the year?

MARJORIE: I don't know the years. It's a very ancient time.

ELAINE: Continue to allow events to unfold. Do you find other women to teach to dance?

MARJORIE: Only when one girl has a friend she wants to bring in. Or if a girl leaves. One of them got married. A man fell in love with her, and he took her as his second wife. We don't really want more than five. We don't have room in the tent.

ELAINE: Tell me about the girls who are with you. What are their names? What is the name of the ten-year-old girl?

MARJORIE: Carey.

ELAINE: And the others? See them individually, one at a time. Feel their presence and know their names.

MARJORIE: Radya. Nadir. Meann. Roselle. Elan. That's all.

ELAINE: Let's move forward now to the next important event. One, two, three. Where are you now? What is happening?

MARJORIE: I'm in the tent. I don't feel very well.

ELAINE: What is wrong?

MARJORIE: I'm weak. There seems to be a dull pain in my stomach. I'm so thin I can see my bones.

ELAINE: Who is with you?

MARJORIE: Carey, only she's grown up.

ELAINE: How do you feel about what's happening?

MARJORIE: I don't really feel anything. I feel detached, like I'm not really there. I don't know what's going on around me. I just feel so vague. I know everything is taken care of, so I just lie there curled up all day.

ELAINE: The women are taking care of you?

MARJORIE: Yes.

ELAINE: Allow events to unfold and tell me what happens.

MARJORIE: I die.

ELAINE: From what perspective are you seeing your death occur? Where are you?

MARJORIE: I'm standing just in front of my body looking down at it.

[*Do not be hesitant to ask questions at the time of someone's death. Death is always a peaceful experience regardless of how the person dies.*]

ELAINE: How do you feel?

MARJORIE: It feels somewhat familiar to be in that situation. I didn't see myself very much. I didn't have a way to see myself . . . I'm not really sure it's me. It just looks like my arms . . . but I know I'm dead and it's all right.

ELAINE: Are there others in spirit there with you?

[*I asked, "Are there others in spirit there with you?" because very often spirit guides or deceased loved ones join the person at the time of death. In our culture we expect nothing to happen at the time of death, so we are surprised to find we still have awareness. It is a very comforting thing for anyone to experience.*]

MARJORIE: Yes. There is one. His name is Dacon.

ELAINE: And who is Dacon?

MARJORIE: He is someone who loves me.

ELAINE: And you will go with Dacon now?

MARJORIE: No, I can't go with him. He lives in another plane or something. He can project himself, and when I die I can be with him for awhile until I go to my next life.

ELAINE: Is Dacon someone you knew in the life you just experienced?

MARJORIE: No. He has never been on earth.

ELAINE: But he is there with you as you cross over into spirit?

MARJORIE: Yes.

ELAINE: And you feel comforted?

MARJORIE: Yes, I missed him.

ELAINE: What happens now?

MARJORIE: We stay at the same place but everything changes around us. It becomes cloudy and vague. We're just alone together in a kind of void. He asks me questions about my last life. I ask him questions. He's so familiar that I feel like I'm in touch with him always. We talk for a long time. He's like my true companion.

ELAINE: Is there anything else you need to be aware of from your contact with Dacon?

MARJORIE: I must remember him while I'm in a body and focused on earth things. I must keep it in the back of my mind that there is always someone who cares.

ELAINE: Let's move now into the highest levels of your own mind, and expanded awareness.

[*Give the one-to-five count.*]

ELAINE: What was the purpose or the lesson learned in the life you have just reviewed?

MARJORIE: The lesson was to not be subservient, to find out that I could take care of myself, could live my own life without having to rely on someone for my physical support. I just wanted to know if I could do it.

ELAINE: Anything else you need to be aware of, any correlation between that life and your present life?

MARJORIE: That my husband is not afraid of my dancing, but of my running away.

ELAINE: How can you help resolve this conflict in your life? How can you help?

MARJORIE: I can tell him that I love him and that nothing will make me run away.

ELAINE: Anything else you need to be aware of?

MARJORIE: My husband is the same man I'm married to now.

ELAINE: I want you to look into the eyes of women you were involved with in that life, those women you helped who then helped you. Look in the eyes of Carey. Who is she now?

MARJORIE: Louise.

ELAINE: And the woman named Radya?

MARJORIE: Yes, that's Elizabeth.

ELAINE: And Nadir?

MARJORIE: That's Jane.

ELAINE: And Mehan?

MARJORIE: Carol.

ELAINE: Roselle?

MARJORIE: Debra.

ELAINE: And your husband in that lifetime? Is he your husband now?

MARJORIE: Yes, we wanted to try one more time to be together. I'm glad that I lived alone, but I'm sad that I hurt him. I would like to make it up.

ELAINE: Any further insight that will help you in your present circumstances?

MARJORIE: It's hard to explain that you can have a fulfilling life without a husband. There is a lot of joy in sisterhood. It's okay to be married and have a nice marriage, but not to ignore sisterhood.

ELAINE: Anything else?

MARJORIE: Not now.

ELAINE: You will have total recall of all you've experienced. In the next few days, in moments of quiet reflection, in reverie, or dreams, if there is additional information that would be helpful to you, it will come into your conscious mind. You will recognize this information and use it in your life. You totally release now at conscious and subconscious levels any negativity or limitations you have brought forward with you into your life. You have opened the door to your own subconscious mind. You are tuned into your own inner guidance. You are aware of the spiritual energy that surrounds you each and every day. You will stay focused on your goals, in tune with yourself, aware of your uniqueness.

[*A one-to-five count given to return the subject to full beta consciousness.*]

When she came out of hypnosis, my client was busy thinking about all she had received. "No wonder he gets so angry with me. He feels like I'm going to run away again. I've been handling this all wrong," she said.

"Do you think you can work this situation out now, knowing what happened in the past?" I asked.

"I think so, I certainly know now what not to say to him."

"Do you know what else is interesting" she said. "The women in that lifetime who lived with me, they're women who are in my dance troupe now. We're beginning to get jobs dancing at women's celebrations. No wonder I care about them all so much."

When I talked with her again several months later she had happy news. Her marriage was now peaceful. She had created a teaching video of her dancing and was also teaching through the community college. Her husband had stopped feeling insecure when she began reassuring him that she would never leave him and telling him how much she loved him. As he became more secure, the tension between them dissolved, and she was free to pursue her dancing and the satisfaction it brought her. She said, "I would never have seen how to work this out, without knowing about that past life."

Again, I could not have guessed what story would unfold as we began. Our answers do lie within us, but we must be still and allow them to come out. Solutions are available, insight can be ours, if we will spend the time looking within.

I have included this next transcript to show that not all regressions are dramatic and full of dialogue. However, this session had great value for the subject. At this time in her life what she needed to know was at a soul level. The woman I was working with has experienced great obstacles in the present. She is a very successful television anchorwoman. Her success is particularly inspiring because when she was eighteen years old she was in an automobile accident that resulted in paraplegia. She accomplishes from a wheelchair what many who have the use of their legs would love to do.

Choosing a Life

[*Trance induced.*]

ELAINE: Your own subconscious mind is choosing the lifetime to explore that most affects your direction and purpose in your present life.

[*Here I used the five-to-one count, continuing to suggest she explore the past-life most affecting her now.*]

ELAINE: Are you inside or outside? What is your first thought or feeling?

DONNA: Outside.

ELAINE: All right. What is it like outside?

DONNA: Foggy.

ELAINE: Are you alone, or is someone else there with you?

DONNA: I'm alone.

ELAINE: Look down at your feet. What are you wearing on your feet?

DONNA: Pointed shoes.

ELAINE: How else are you dressed? What are you wearing?

DONNA: Scarves. Like scarves from a hat.

ELAINE: You're female?

DONNA: Yes.

ELAINE: How old are you?

DONNA: I'm young . . . a young adult.

ELAINE: Tell me about this particular day. Allow this day to unfold. What is significant about this particular day? You're outside and it's foggy. What's happening?

[As part of my question I summarized what she has told me thus far to help her receive more information.]

DONNA: Well, I'm just walking outside of this house. And there's a stone fence. And I'm waiting for someone.

ELAINE: Let's move forward in time to when the person you're waiting for arrives. One, two, three. What is happening now?

DONNA: I'm talking to a man. An old man.

ELAINE: How do you feel as you talk with him?

DONNA: Like he's somehow releasing me from this prison. He knows how to get me out.

ELAINE: Have you been restrained or locked up? What kind of prison is he releasing you from?

DONNA: It's not a prison, it's a house, but I don't get to go out.

ELAINE: But he has a way for you to be able to do that?

DONNA: Yes.

ELAINE: Make yourself aware of the house and your connection to this house. What do you do there? Why are you kept there? Move back in time to the event that will make that clear to you. Three, two, one. What is happening?

DONNA: I don't know. I'm doing something in these little clothes washers. But I don't want to be there.

ELAINE: Are you a servant?

DONNA: I was a servant, but I'm no longer one.

ELAINE: Make yourself aware of the old man you were talking to on the day you were standing outside the house. Be aware of him and your connection to him. Why will he help you?

DONNA: He's like a grandfather, but I didn't know he was around.

ELAINE: How do you feel about him?

DONNA: Like he offers some hope because we're related. I don't know. He's trying to help me. But I don't really want to go. I've carved out this life, but I have to go.

ELAINE: Are you fearful of not knowing what will happen in new circumstances?

DONNA: Yes. It's a boring life.

ELAINE: How do you respond to his offer of help?

DONNA: Yes. I accept it.

ELAINE: Move forward to the time you act upon whatever he's suggesting will free you from these circumstances. One, two, three. Where are you now? What is happening?

DONNA: I'm not there.

ELAINE: Where do you find yourself now?

DONNA: In a city.

ELAINE: So your circumstances have changed. You are away from that house?

DONNA: Yes.

ELAINE: Where is the old man? Is he in the city with you?

DONNA: No, I'm with friends.

ELAINE: Continue to allow events to unfold and tell me what happens now. You're in the city with friends.

DONNA: I feel totally different.

ELAINE: In what way?

DONNA: Like I'm a new person.

ELAINE: How will you take care of yourself? How will you see to your needs? Move forward. Allow yourself to be aware.

DONNA: I'm riding in this big empty arena. I'm older.

ELAINE: You're riding a horse?

DONNA: No.

[*I have misunderstood what she was saying. She corrects me, but I am confused about just what is happening. I continue asking questions, trying to clarify what is going on.*]

ELAINE: Writing with a pen?

DONNA: Yes.

ELAINE: What are you writing? What is the purpose of the writing?

DONNA: It's like I'm at a fight.

ELAINE: Like a boxing match, something of that sort?

DONNA: Yeah. People are coming to fight.

ELAINE: Who do you write for? Are you employed as a writer?

DONNA: Yes.

ELAINE: Do you work for a newspaper?

DONNA: I don't know. Maybe a publication house, or something. There's an old man that looks something like that grandfather.

ELAINE: How do you feel about the writing?

DONNA: It's good, but it's not quite what I want.

ELAINE: What is your name? Hear it spoken.

DONNA: Well, they call me Sarah. But I'm older. I look forty something.

ELAINE: How do you feel about your life now?

DONNA: Like it's half there.

ELAINE: You don't have everything you want now?

DONNA: I have a fur. But I don't want a fur.

ELAINE: So you've done well for yourself monetarily?

DONNA: Yes.

ELAINE: Let's move forward now to the next significant

event in the lifetime you're exploring as Sarah. One, two, three. Where are you now? What is happening?

[*I have a feeling she has gone to a different life, so I direct her to continue exploring the life as Sarah.*]

DONNA: Now I'm all alone and I'm in this little life raft.

ELAINE: Are you still Sarah?

[*Now I specifically ask if she is still Sarah. The regression is very disjointed and I'm feeling confused about what she's receiving.*]

ELAINE: What are you doing in the life raft? How did you get there?

DONNA: I took a trip. I tried to get away. Something happened. I tried to save myself and I got in this life raft.

ELAINE: Were you on a ship that you had to abandon?

DONNA: I think so because I have my little travel case with me still. I have dressy clothes on, not like what I'd wear in a life raft. It's very small. I'm just hoping someone will find me.

[*I have omitted the remainder of the regression. She continued to answer very briefly. I asked every question I could think of to try to get a clearer picture of what was happening. Finally, at the end of the life she was exploring, since I felt she needed further insight, I directed her to another lifetime. The following are her responses. They are the heart of the matter.*]

ELAINE: Move now to another lifetime that will give you insight and understanding into your present life and circumstances. Move to another lifetime that will give you insight into the purpose you have designed for yourself in this lifetime.

DONNA: It's a window of light. It's very bright. So bright I can hardly see.

ELAINE: Are you male or female?

DONNA: I don't know.

ELAINE: What are you looking at out the window?

DONNA: Just a lot of images.

ELAINE: Why are you there?

DONNA: I don't know.

ELAINE: Move to an important time. One, two, three. What is happening now?

DONNA: I'm sitting up very high with a lot of clouds around me. With a young man in very bright funny clothes.

ELAINE: How do you feel?

DONNA: Oh, he's great.

ELAINE: What's important about this particular time?

DONNA: Because I'm choosing my life. And I can have anything.

ELAINE: Are you between lives?

[*By her answers, she is obviously not on earth in a physical body. I ask her specifically if she is "between lives". If your subjects need insight from the time "between lives" without direction from you, they will explore this time. The information received is very similar to what has been reported in the study of near-death experiences. Common factors in a near-death experience and time with master beings between lives are the intense white light and the profound knowledge gained.*]

DONNA: I think so.

ELAINE: Be aware of the presence of any others who are there with you at this gathering when you are choosing the circumstances for your life. Feel the presence of any others who are there.

DONNA: There's lots of them there.

ELAINE: Are they helping you make the decisions about your life?

DONNA: Yes. But I have to decide.

ELAINE: The choice is yours to make?

DONNA: Yes.

ELAINE: What choices do you make for yourself?

DONNA: I have to be challenged more than ever before. I have to be stimulated more than ever before. That's why it's so hard to decide.

ELAINE: Is this the meeting prior to your present life as Donna?

DONNA: Maybe.

ELAINE: Which life are you planning? On the count of three you'll be aware. One, two, three. Which life are you planning?

DONNA: Now.

ELAINE: So you needed circumstances that would be very challenging and very stimulating in your present life?

DONNA: Yes.

ELAINE: And how do you decide to create those challenges and that stimulation?

DONNA: I look over everything on earth, and I pick and choose what I like and what I don't like. Some people tell me some of the options and that helps me. But it's a heavy decision, because it has to be grandiose.

ELAINE: What other guidance or direction are you given as you make these decisions?

DONNA: My mother helps me.

ELAINE: She will be your mother in this life?

DONNA: Yes. She helps me decide.

ELAINE: Any other input from those you will know or whose lives you will touch in this incarnation as Donna?

DONNA: There are just so many people. They're all helping me plan this. Just experienced souls.

ELAINE: They are guiding and assisting you in making these decisions?

DONNA: Yes.

ELAINE: If you were to ask one of them for guidance or input into your life at this particular time, what guidance would they give you?

DONNA: That above all . . . remember, they just keep telling me, you're a leader, you'll always rise above it. I mean I don't believe this, but they're telling me.

ELAINE: What else are they telling you?

DONNA: I guess I'm doing it for everybody. That makes my palms sweaty, because I just don't know if I'm ready for it. Everybody keeps saying, "Yes you are."

ELAINE: What else do you need to be aware of from that meeting, that planning?

DONNA: I'm supposed to . . . I'm not supposed to forget to live that life while I'm there, even though I'm going to be so busy. It's okay, and it's supposed to be a part of my life. They're telling me that. There's just so much to do. But everybody else is totally convinced that I'm the right person, so I'm just preparing myself for it.

ELAINE: Anything else you need to be aware of?

DONNA: It's like I have these two jobs, and I just want to do the one. But I just need, I guess, to become embroiled in this life, and to me that . . I don't know.

ELAINE: So it will be a busy life, and you are to live it fully?

DONNA: Yes. I'm telling them I don't know if I can do that. I can do anything but that. They're telling me I should do both.

ELAINE: How can you best achieve a life with balance?

DONNA: I'll know lots of people. I'm to let myself feel what they're feeling. Get in touch that way. And that's the part that I'm standing away from. I don't want to, or I can't do it.

ELAINE: And yet this is one of the things you are to accomplish in this life?

DONNA: That's what I've been told.

ELAINE: How can you best achieve that?

DONNA: To let go.

ELAINE: Do you need to listen to your intuition more, to flow with the universal plan for your life?

DONNA: Yes. But I need to loosen my grasp.

ELAINE: How can you best accomplish that?

DONNA: It's internal, but it's through the people I'm in

contact with. But again, it's just letting go of that mission. I can't hold on too tightly to that. Do what I have to do.

ELAINE: How can you keep yourself mindful of that in the present?

DONNA: I'm not sure. I'm ready to find out. I'm on the edge.

ELAINE: All right. I want you to be back with those highly evolved, loving spirits who helped you to plan this life. Feel their presence once again and ask for their guidance once again about how you can best accomplish maintaining the balance in the present. What direction are you given?

DONNA: To let my guard down. This invisible distance I have around me. Just to let it down. Just be trusting and not play it so safe.

ELAINE: Anything else you need to be aware of that would be helpful to you?

DONNA: It's very important. Now I know what they mean. I need to keep Nature in my mind and be a part of Nature. If not, I can never accomplish what I'm trying to accomplish. And the balance—I need to go to it, be with it, in order for this balance to take place.

ELAINE: Is there anything else you need to be aware of now, any other guidance from your higher mind, from your own masters and guides, that would be helpful to you in the present?

DONNA: That window of light. It's there in those nature settings, and that's why I have to be there, for that light. It's like tremendous energy. I have to go and find it.

ELAINE: Anything else?

DONNA: No.

ELAINE: You will have total, vivid recall of everything you've experienced. You will totally release at conscious and subconscious levels all negativity or limitations from the lifetime you have reviewed, or any other lifetime that might limit you in the present. You bring forward with you into your present life all of the knowledge, wisdom, and understanding gained from this experience. You are totally open to your own intuition, your own inner guidance. You are aware at every level of the plan for your life, of your ability to execute that plan and to live your life in a very balanced and whole way. You will find yourself now in the next weeks and months and years intuitively turning to nature for that balance, seeking out teachers who can help you know of the magic of nature and the balance available there. You will find yourself completely aligned with the energy of the earth you live on, in balance with the universe, knowing you are an integral part of it all, that your inner self, your inner guidance, has validity. You are completely open and receptive now to your own intuition, your own guidance and awareness. You will bring forward with you into your present life all of the knowledge, wisdom, and understanding gained by having this expanded state of consciousness, by tapping into the reservoirs of peace and perfection within yourself.

[*The one-to-five count given to return the subject to full beta consciousness.*]

This is the kind of session that makes my life interesting and my work fulfilling. The guidance Donna received from master beings between lives gave her invaluable insight into her circumstances. She has already turned catastrophic events into opportunities. Nothing happens without reason, no turn of events should become a stopping place in life. Everything we experience is an opportunity for growth. We can trust the guidance available to us. It is limitless.

CHAPTER 14

The Beginning

When I was a child, my mother told me, "Everything you learn will always be yours. Regardless of the circumstances in your life, whether you do or don't have money in the bank, what you learn can never be taken from you." Those words have been a compelling force in my life.

For many years I experienced frustration in my work, divided between teaching self-hypnosis to some clients and using hypnosis with other clients to help them recall past lives. I tried self-hypnosis for the first time more than twenty years ago to help me with the birth of my second child. I was the world's original skeptic and thought there was no possible way self-hypnosis could allow me to experience perfectly comfortable, pain-free childbirth. Much to my surprise, the hypnosis worked amazingly well. I got up from the delivery table and walked back to my room. The next morning I went home, feeling wonderful. And so, when I began my business, I taught self-hypnosis. I knew how incredibly important and useful that tool is.

The first formal training I received was in the use of hypnosis to recall past lives. That was followed by many workshops by a wide variety of instructors. I have spent most of my life asking questions, always wondering what else I could do, what else I could learn.

So half my work consisted of teaching self-hypnosis. The other half consisted of working with clients to guide them through past lives, both in groups and privately. But I always felt an undercurrent of discomfort about my work. When clients came to learn self-hypnosis simply to be more effective as public speakers, or to quit smoking, or whatever, I was not content. But when they came to experience a regression, I was also not content. I felt that each set of clients was being cheated of other knowledge I had. And then, one golden day, it finally dawned on me that I could teach people to do both—to achieve an altered state of consciousness and to explore their past lives. One discipline enhances the other. They weave together perfectly.

I believe that our minds have great potential to heal, to explain, and to guide us through the labyrinth. The trick is to allow understanding to come into focus, to know in our hearts that we have found a key to our own inner workings. I encourage you to trust, to explore, to experiment, to expand your horizons beyond your wildest imaginings. It is so beautiful to come to an understanding of why we are the way we are, and then to use that understanding to make fundamental changes within our hearts and souls. The tools presented in this book will give you the power to do that.

Look at your life. There are times when all the old answers no longer work, times when you find yourself searching for more: you can feel the shift in direction. This is an excellent time to begin exploring your own past, your own soul-history.

We are not just our physical bodies. We are also our mind, our emotions, our spirituality. We are all of these things, and every part of us will be affected as we travel through our past lives. Know that as you work with this new knowledge, more and more information will come to you, more and more understanding. You are your own best teacher. You have chosen the lessons to be learned. They are yours. They belong to no one else.

It is so important to accept yourself as you are now, right this minute. Give yourself credit for all the wonderful things that make you a unique person. Acknowledge your inner beauty and your external imperfections. Know that you are a masterpiece in the making. It is also important as you travel through this awareness to keep a journal. Make notes, write about how you feel as you progress. It will serve an important function in your life. It will be your map to the center of yourself; your path that leads you to the edge of the abyss, and your wings to fly.

Without this inward journey, there is no focal point to our lives. We stay scattered, unable to know our purpose.

I firmly believe there is a plan to our lives, there is a reason, there is purpose.

It lies within our power to understand the lessons we have created for ourselves, to live our life with a clear idea of why we're here. The past is a key to the present. You now hold this key in your hand.

It is yours.

I promise.

Resources

I have learned the most from people who have studied a wide variety of disciplines, who do not limit themselves to a narrow view of the world. You will probably be able to add titles to this list.

Reincarnation—an Overview

These books give an in-depth look at the subject of reincarnation. They are extremely well done, an extensive collection of great thinkers from every discipline.

Cranston, Sylvia, and Carey Williams. *Reincarnation: A New Horizon in Science, Religion, and Society.* New York: Julian Press, 1984.

Fisher, Joe. *The Case for Reincarnation* (Preface by the Dalai Lama). New York: Bantam, 1987.

Head, Joseph, and S. L. Cranston, eds. *Reincarnation: The Phoenix Fire Mystery.* New York: Julian Press/Crown, 1984.

Reincarnation—Case Histories

These books are accounts of past-life regressions and the profound effects experienced by the subjects, valuable background information about why one would choose to explore past lives.

Fiore, Edith. *You Have Been Here Before*. New York: Ballentine, 1979.

Sparrow, Lynn Elwell. *Reincarnation: Claiming Your Past, Creating Your Future*. San Francisco: Harper & Row, 1988.

Sutphen, Dick. *Past Lives, Future Loves*. New York: Pocket Books, 1982.

———. *You Were Born Again to Be Together*. New York: Pocket Books, 1976.

Wambach, Helen. *Reliving Past Lives*. New York: Barnes & Noble, 1978.

Weiss, Brian. *Many Lives, Many Masters*. New York: Simon & Schuster/Fireside, 1988.

Imagery and Visualization

These books are excellent resources for understanding and using the creative part of the mind to make changes in one's life.

Gawain, Shakti. *Creative Visualization*. New York: Bantam, 1982.

Samuels, Mike, and Nancy Samuels. *Seeing With the Mind's Eye*. New York: Random House, 1975.

Tools from Other Times for Now

These tools will help stimulate right brain awareness. Their source is ancient; the knowledge has been distilled for our use in the present.

Blum, Ralph. *The Book of Runes*. New York: St. Martin's Press, 1988.

Greer, Mary. *Tarot Constellations*. North Hollywood, California: Newcastle, 1987.

Sams, Jamie, and David Carson. *Medicine Cards*. Santa Fe: Bear & Co., 1988.

Using the Mind for Healing and Wellness

The human mind is a powerful resource that can be used in our lives for healing. These books give an understanding of the body/mind connection and techniques to use for healing.

Hay, Louise. *You Can Heal Your Life*. Santa Monica, California: Hay House, 1984.

Siegel, Bernie. *Love, Medicine & Miracles*. New York: Harper & Row, 1986.

Simonton, O. Carl. *Getting Well Again*. New York: J. P. Tarcher, 1978.

Writing—A Way to Understand Yourself

A wonderful book that will help you know the importance of each experience, and encourage you to write it down—an important part of living with awareness.

Goldberg, Natalie. *Writing Down the Bones*. Boston: Shambhala, 1986.

Music on Cassette Audiotapes

As you practice self-hypnosis techniques, you may find it helpful to listen to this kind of music. Steven Halpern terms his music "the anti-frantic alternative." It is designed to create a deep sense of relaxation.

Allan, Laura, et. al. *Reflections*. San Rafael, CA: Sound Rx SRx 3002.

Halpern, Steven. *Spectrum Suite*. San Rafael, CA: Sound Rx SRx 7770.

Halpern, Steven, and Daniel Kobialka. *Recollections.* San Rafael, CA: Sound Rx 7823.

Halpern, Steven, and Georgia Kelly. *Ancient Echoes.* San Rafael, CA: Sound Rx SRx 7783.